"I believe with complete faith in the coming of Mashiach. Though he tarry, nonetheless I await him every day, that he will come."

Principles of the Faith, No. 12

MASHIACH

The Principle of Mashiach and the Messianic Era in Jewish Law and Tradition

by
Jacob Immanuel Schochet

Expanded Edition

Published by

S. I. E.
New York - Toronto

5752 - 1992

First edition.... July 1991
Second edition... September 1991
Third edition... April 1992

Copyright © 1992 by J. Immanuel Schochet

All rights reserved. No part of this publication may be reproduced in any form or by any means, including photocopying and translation, without permission in writing from the copyright holder or the publisher.

Published and Distributed by

S. I. E.

788 Eastern Parkway
Brooklyn N.Y 11213
(718) 778-5436

55 Charleswood Drive
Downsview Ont. M3H1X5
(416) 636-9709

5752 - 1992

ISBN 1-8814-0000-X
Library of Congress Catalog Card Number: 92-90728

Contents

Foreword 5

Foreword to Second Edition 11
Foreword to Third Edition 12

I   The Belief in Mashiach 17

II   The Messianic Era 19
     A. Restoration of the *Bet Hamikdash*
     B. Ingathering of the Exiles of Israel
     C. End to Evil and Sins
     D. Awareness and Knowledge of G-d
     E. Universal Worship of G-d
     F. Universal Peace and Harmony
     G. Resurrection of the Dead
     H. Blissful Utopia: End to Disease and Death

III   *Ikvot Meshicha:*
     The Time Immediately Before Mashiach 34

IV   The Personality of Mashiach 37
     A. Mashiach – Human
     B. Mashiach in Every Generation
     C. The Character and Qualities of Mashiach

V   Date of Mashiach's Coming 45

VI   Hastening the Coming of Mashiach 48
     A. Special *Mitzvot*
     B. Unity of Israel

VII   Awaiting Mashiach 54
     A. The Obligation to Await
     B. *Kivuy:* The Merit and Effect of Awaiting
     C. Demanding Mashiach

VIII Now – More Than Ever! 65

Supplements 69

Bibliography 103

Foreword

We live in cataclysmic times, an age of drastic changes and fast-moving developments in all aspects of the human condition. They reflect with uncanny preciseness the symptoms of the advent of the Messianic era, acutely defined in the Talmud, Midrash, and other sacred writings.[1] This has made people ever more aware of the principle of the Messianic redemption – the concept of Mashiach and the effects of his imminent revelation.

The belief in the coming of Mashiach is fundamental to the Torah and the Jewish Faith.[2] Very few, however, delve into its meaning and implications. The doctrine is affirmed, but more as an abstract theorem than a practical issue of immediate relevance. Indeed, great apprehension surrounds this subject. This apprehension is fed partly by an innate fear of the unknown, the confounding mystery of a hidden future. Moreover, there is the memory of the sad consequences of Messianic misadventures of the past, such as the unfortunate history of pseudo-

---

1. See below, ch. III.
2. See below, ch. I; and ch. VII, sect. A.

Messiahs and unrealized predictions which left a trail of painful disillusion and dismay.[3]

On the other hand, precisely in times of great trials and tribulations – over-abundant in Jewish history, to this very day – it is belief in Mashiach and the *ge'ulah* (redemption) that kindles the sparks of hope. It has helped overcome the worst persecutions and sufferings in anticipation of the Divine Day of Judgment when good will triumph over evil, and the world will enter the utopian era when truth, peace and universal brotherhood will reign supreme as "the whole earth shall be full of knowledge of G-d" (Isaiah 11:9) and "all shall call upon the Name of G-d to serve Him with one accord." (Zephaniah 3:9)[4]

The symptoms of the Messianic age encompass us now as never before. This has renewed interest for more knowledge about it. Questions are asked, but there are few sources that bring together the information scattered over the many writings of the sacred Scriptures, Talmud and Midrashim. Of these few, hardly any are available in the vernacular or in terms amenable to the average layman's understanding.

In this context, the author was asked recently to deliver some lectures on this topic. These

---

3. *Cf. Sanhedrin* 97b "Blasted be those that calculate the end; for (people) would say, since (that time for) the end has been reached and (Mashiach) has not come – he will never come. Rather, wait for him.." (See *Margaliyot Hayam, ad loc.;* and Rambam's *Igeret Teyman,* ed. Kapach, ch. 3, for different versions in the wording of this condemnation.) *Cf. Igeret Teyman,* ch. 3; and below, ch. V, note 75.

4. See below, ch. II, sect. D and E.

were followed by numerous requests to commit them to writing. That is how this book came about: a synopsis of those lectures.

The reader should not expect anything original, nor a fully exhaustive treatment. At best there is some effort to present a limited compilation of basic principles about Mashiach and the Messianic era, culled from *Tnach,* Talmud, Midrashim and Rambam, and a few other authoritative sources, relevant to an overall understanding of our subject.

Even so, the effort that went into committing these teachings to writing was not for mere academic reasons. Knowledge is itself a means toward a higher end: "the purpose of wisdom is *teshuvah* (return to G-d) and *ma'asim tovim* (good deeds)." *(Berachot* 17a*)* Thus it is hoped that a study of these pages will not only inform, but also make the reader realize the relevant actuality of their contents: to awaken or strengthen the anticipation of the Messianic redemption as ordained by *halachah* (Jewish law).5

Ours is not the first age that has been identified as most auspicious for the realization of the Messianic prophecies. When such occasions arose before, the sages of the time spoke out orally and in writing, urging the people to better their ways and to avail themselves of the opportunity to bring Mashiach. For example, R. Mosheh ben Nachman (Ramban) wrote his *Sefer Hage'ulah* in anticipation of the redemption in his days. To still greater extent, R. Yitzchak Abarbanel calculated the same for his

---

5. See below, ch. VII.

own time and composed (to this day the most comprehensive works on our topic) *Mashmi'a Yeshu'ah* (a compilation of all the Messianic prophecies of the *Tnach*, except for those in the Book of Daniel), *Mayanei Hayeshu'ah* (an extensive commentary on Daniel), and *Yeshu'ot Meshicho* (discussing the Messianic passages of our sages, and refuting some distortions about the principle of Mashiach).

Abarbanel notes that he composed his work out of concern for his people "in the night of its darkness, to awaken it from the sleep of its *galut*.. Because of the afflictions of G-d's people, its heart warmed and thirsts for the waters of the soul.. thus I dug this well to offer my chosen people 'cold water for a faint soul, good news..' (Proverbs 25:25).."[6] "My whole purpose is to strengthen feeble hands and fortify stumbling feet.."[7] Like Ramban before him,[8] he regards his venture of calculating the *ketz* (the Messianic end), and otherwise revealing and explicating the meaning and intent of Messianic passages, not only permissible but obligatory, because of the proximity of the redemption.[9] Thus he posits that in view of the imminent *ge'ulah*, all those who act in this vein

> "make the many meritorious, because they strengthen G-d's people in their faith, add hope and immense anticipation of the Divine Grace.. (as they realize that) 'My salvation is near to come and My

---

6. *Mayanei Hayeshu'ah*, Introduction, s.v. *kamti*.
7. *Ibid.*, concluding paragraph of the book.
8. See below, ch. V, note 75.
9. *Mayanei Hayeshu'ah*, Mayan I: ch. 2.

> righteousness to be revealed' (Isaiah 56:1)."[10]

In the past century this happened again through the sainted R. Israel Meir Hakohen, the most widely acclaimed authority of his day, better known by the title of his famous work *Chafetz Chaim*. He spoke, wrote, urged and admonished the people of Israel incessantly to ready itself for the imminent redemption. Like perhaps none before him, he issued letters and proclamations, and published special works to awaken Israel to that message. He innovated a renewal of the study of laws relating to the Temple-service, especially by *kohanim*, as this would soon be of practical relevance.[11]

For whatever reasons, these potentials were not yet actualized.[12] Nowadays, however, current events again indicate, even more than before, that

> "The voice of my beloved, behold he has come, leaping over mountains, skipping over hills.. Behold, he is standing behind our wall, watching through the windows, peering through the lattices.. Arise my loved one, my fair one, and go forth! For behold, the winter is over, the rain is over

---

10. *Ibid.*
11. See especially his *Tzipita Liyeshu'ah*, and *Ma'amar Torah Or* (the lengthy introduction to his edition of *Assifat Zekenim* on *Kadashim*); and the quotation from *Chizuk Emunah*, cited below, ch. VII-A. Excerpts from many of his proclamations and statements can be found in the anthologies of his comments on the Torah and the Siddur.
12. See below, ch. V, note 75.

and gone. The blossoms have appeared on earth, the time of singing has arrived, and the voice of the guide is heard in the land!"

Song of Songs 2:8-12

The great leaders of our own generation are once again urging that we are living in most auspicious, momentous times. Thus it is incumbent to renew our belief in, and anticipation of, the Messianic redemption: to be aware of what it means, to study the relevant laws and teachings, to ask for and await its immediate realization – thereby bringing it about in actuality.[13] Furtherance of this goal is the ultimate objective of this book.

J. Immanuel Schochet

Toronto Ont., 28 Sivan 5751

---

13. See below, ch. VIII, note 131. *Cf. Mayanei Hayeshu'ah* I:2: "He who really cares (lit., it touches his heart) will make an effort to find out what will be in the 'end', when that *ketz* of wonders will be, 'seek it as silver and search for it as for hidden treasures' (par. Proverbs 2:4)."

Foreword to Second Edition

The reception of this work was overwhelming, necessitating a second edition so shortly after the first one. This indicates not only the immense desire for knowledge about the important principle of Mashiach but also an ever-increasing awakening of the Halachically required anticipation of his long-awaited coming.

In response to numerous requests, I complemented this new edition by adding (a) a translation of Rambam's legal rulings about the principle of Mashiach and the Messianic era (the last two chapters of his *Mishneh Torah*), with brief notes of sources and explanations; and (b) a short sketch of the little known concept of "Mashiach ben Yossef." This new edition also provided an opportunity to correct typographical errors and to insert omissions.

No doubt but that the study of the Torah's teachings about Mashiach and the Messianic era will hasten their fulfillment, in the literal sense, that we may merit this most speedily on the level of our empirical reality.[1]

J. Immanuel Schochet

Toronto Ont., 18 Elul 5751

---

1. See *Tanchuma*, Tzav:14.

Foreword to Third Edition

The gratifying need for a new edition provides a welcome opportunity to correct a few more errors and to insert some additional omissions.

This third edition appears, Providentially, in the auspicious month of Nissan, when we celebrate and relive the first redemption of Israel from its first *galut*. Pondering and sensing the events of the exodus from Egypt, with all their implications, leads to freedom from all forms of personal *galut;* and that, in turn, is a prelude to sensing, anticipating and actualizing the Messianic redemption for all of Israel.[1] May we merit to experience this speedily in our very own days, as our sages said, "In Nissan they were redeemed [in the past], and in Nissan they will be redeemed in the time to come"[2] – with the

---

1. See *Sefer Ba'al Shem Tov,* Bereishit:par. 166 and note 143; *ibid.,* Shemot: par. 5-6, and note 4. Note *Bereishit Rabba* 16:4, that the Egyptian exile is the compounding root of all subsequent exiles; and *Zohar* II:216b-217a, that the redemption from Egypt is the compounding root for all subsequent redemptions, including the Messianic redemption.
2. *Rosh Hashanah* 11a; *Zohar* III:249a.

fulfillment of the prophecy, "As in the days of your going out from the land of Egypt, I will show them wondrous things!" (Michah 7:15)

As this new edition coincides with the momentous occasion of the 90th birthday[3] of the revered Lubavitcher Rebbe, R. Menachem M. Schneerson שליט"א, I humbly dedicate it to his merit, with prayerful wishes that Almighty God bless him with many more years in good and full health, strength and happiness: "I will satiate him with length of days amd will let him see My salvation!" (Psalms 91:16) May he merit, alongside all of Israel, the speedy fulfillment of "The ransomed of G-d shall return and come to Zion with singing and everlasting joy upon their heads; they shall obtain gladness and joy, and sorrow and sighing shall flee away." (Isaiah 35:10 and 51:12)

J. Immanuel Schochet

11th of Nissan 5752

---

3. On the religious significance of birthdays see my *"Beyom Tovah Heyei Betov,"* in *Gevurato Shel Torah* (Toronto Ont., 1983), pp. 69-86. On the special significance of the age of ninety, see R. Yitzchak Dov-Ber of Liadi, *Sidur Tefilah im Perush Maharid*, vol. II, p. 191.

אשרי אדם שזכו לו אבותיו,
אשרי אדם שיש לו יתד במי להתלות בה
(ירושלמי, ברכות פ"ד ה"א)

לאמי מורתי
אשת חבר מנב"ת הרבנית
מרת **שרה שאשא** שתליט"א
עוד ינובון בשיבה דשנים ורעננים יהיו
(תהלים צב, טו. וע"פ מל"ד ורד"ק שם)

MASHIACH

**The Principle of Mashiach and the
Messianic Era
in Jewish Law and Tradition**

I. The Belief in Mashiach

The belief in the coming of Mashiach and the Messianic redemption is one of the fundamental principles of the Jewish faith.[1] Every Jew must believe that Mashiach will arise and restore the Kingdom of David to its original state and sovereignty, rebuild the *Bet Hamikdash* (Holy Temple of Jerusalem), gather the dispersed of Israel, and in his days all the laws of the Torah shall be reinstituted as they had been aforetimes.[2]

> Whoever does not believe in him, or whoever does not look forward to (and anticipate) his coming, denies not only [the words of] the other prophets but also [those of] the *Torah* [the Five Books of Moses] and of Moses our Teacher! For the *Torah* testifies about him, as it is said: "G-d, your G-d, will return your captivity and have compassion on you. He will return and gather you.. If your dispersed be in the utmost end of the heavens.. G-d will bring you.." (Deuteronomy 30:3-5) These words, explicitly stated in the

---

1. Rambam, Principles of the Faith, Article 12.
2. Rambam, *Hilchot Melachim* 11:1

Torah, compound all the things spoken by all the prophets.[3]

Some authorities view this principle as an integral part of the first of the Ten Commandments ("I am G-d, your G-d, who has taken you out of the land of Egypt, from the house of bondage;" Exodus 20:2), which charges us with the belief in G-d, i.e.,

> "to know that He who created heaven and earth is the sole ruler above and below and in all four directions.. This includes.. [the principle] that man is asked in his judgment after death, 'Did you long for salvation?' The Scriptural source for this obligation is compounded in the above: just as we must believe that G-d took us out of Egypt, as it is written, 'I am G-d, your G-d, who has taken you out from the land of Egypt' .. so I want that you believe that I am G-d, your G-d, who will yet gather you and save you.."[4]

---

3. *Ibid.* See below, ch. VII-A.
4. R. Yitzchak of Corbeil, *Semak,* par. 1. See below, ch. VII-A.

II. The Messianic Era

A. Restoration of the *Bet Hamikdash*

Mashiach shall restore the *Bet Hamikdash* in Jerusalem.[5] This refers to the third *Bet Hamikdash* that will stand forever, in fulfillment of the Divine prophecy of Ezekiel 37:26-28: "I shall give My Sanctuary in their midst forever. My dwelling-place shall be over them .. The nations shall know that I am G-d who sanctifies Israel,

---

5. From some sources it appears that Mashiach will build the third *Bet Hamikdash* (*Vayikra Rabba* 9:6; *Bamidbar Rabba* 13:2; *Shir Rabba* end of ch. 4 etc.; followed by Rambam, *Hilchot Melachim* 11:1 and 4). From other sources it follows that the third *Bet Hamikdash* is built by the Almighty Himself (*Zohar* I:28a, 114a, 183b and III:221a etc. [and *cf. Zohar* II:240b!]; followed by Rashi and Tossafot on *Sukah* 41a, *Rosh Hashanah* 30a, and *Shevu'ot* 15b). *Cf. Torah Shelemah*, Beshalach 15:17 (especially note 211); and *Sha'arei Zohar* on *Sukah* 41a (see there; and R. Menachem M. Schneerson *shalita*, *Likkutei Sichot* Vol. XI, p. 98 note 61; Vol. XVII, p. 418; and Vol. XXVII, p. 204f.; for ways to reconcile the two views).

when My Sanctuary shall be in the midst of them forever."[6]

B. Ingathering of the Exiles of Israel

Through Mashiach shall be effected the ingathering of all the exiles of Israel:[7]

Deuteronomy 30:3-4: "G-d, your G-d, shall bring back your captivity .. and He will return and gather you from all the nations whither G-d, your G-d, has scattered you. If your banished shall be at the utmost end of the heavens, G-d, your G-d, shall gather you from there, and He shall take you from there."

Isaiah 11:11-12,16: "It shall be on that day that G-d shall again set His hand for a second time to acquire the remnant of His people that shall remain from Assyria and from Egypt, from Pathros and from Cush and from Elam, from Shinar and from Chamat and from the islands of the sea.. There shall be a highway for the remnant of His people that shall remain from Assyria, as there was for Israel on the day they went up from the land of Egypt."

Isaiah 43:5-6: "Fear not, for I am with you; I will bring your seed from the east and gather you from the west. I shall say to the north, 'Give up,' and to the south, 'Do not hold back, bring My sons from far and My daughters from the end of the earth.'"

---

6. See also Ezekiel ch. 40*ff.*; and *cf.* Isaiah 2:2*f.* cited below ch. II-E.

7. See *Bereishit Rabba* 98:9; *Midrash Hagadol* on Genesis 49:11.

Amos 9:14-15: "I shall return the captivity of My people Israel and they shall build the waste cities and settle .. I shall plant them upon their land, and they shall no more be plucked out of their land that I have given them, says G-d, your G-d."

Jeremiah 23:7-8: "Therefore behold, days shall come, says G-d, that they shall no longer say, 'As G-d lives who has taken up the children of Israel from the land of Egypt;' but 'As G-d lives who has taken up and brought the seed of the House of Israel from the north country and from all the countries where He had banished them,' and they shall dwell in their land."

Ezekiel 39:25, 27-29: "..Now I shall bring back the captivity of Jacob and I shall have compassion on the whole House of Israel, and I shall be zealous for My holy Name .. When I shall have returned them from the nations and gathered them from the lands of their enemies.. They shall know that I am G-d, their G-d, in that I exiled them to the nations and gathered them unto their land, and I will not leave any one of them there. I will no more hide My face from them, as I will pour out My spirit upon the House of Israel..".[8]

The Ten Tribes of the Northern Kingdom of Israel, exiled by the Assyrians before the destruction of the first *Bet Hamikdash* (II-Kings, ch. 17), and dispersed beyond the river

---

8. Additional sources for the ingathering of the exiles are: Isaiah 27:12, 49:8-9, and 60:4; Jeremiah 30:2 and 31:7; Ezekiel 34:11-13 and 37:21; Zechariah 8:7-8; etc.

Sambation and the 'Mountains of Darkness,' will also return.[9]

This Divine promise of the return and restoration of Israel is unconditional. It will occur even if the people should not want to return:

> "That which arises in your mind shall not come to pass, namely that which you say, 'We shall be like the nations, like the families of the countries, to serve wood and stone.' As I live, says the Lord G-d, I shall surely rule over them with a mighty hand and with an outstretched arm and with fury poured out. I shall take you out from the nations and gather you from the lands in which you were scattered, with a mighty hand, an outstretched arm and with fury poured out.. I shall pass you under the rod and bring you into the covenant.. For on My holy mountain, on the mountain of the height of Israel, says the Lord G-d, there shall all of the whole House of Israel serve Me .. when I bring you out from the nations and gather you from the lands where you were scattered, and I shall be sanctified in you in the eyes of the nations. You shall know that I am G-d when I bring you to the earth of Israel, to the land about which I raised My hand to give it to your fathers." (Ezekiel 20:32-37, 40-42)

---

9. *Sanhedrin* 110b; *Bamidbar Rabba* 16:25; *Tanchuma*, ed. Buber, Shlach-Hossafot:6 (and see the editor's notes there); *Pesikta Rabaty* 32:10 (ed. Friedmann, ch. 31). *Cf.* Ramban, *Sefer Hage'ulah*, sha'ar I.

"Therefore say to the House of Israel, Thus said the Lord G-d: I am not doing (this) for your sake, House of Israel, but for My holy Name which you profaned among the nations wither you came. I shall sanctify My great Name that was profaned among the nations, that you profaned in their midst, and the nations shall know that I am G-d, says the Lord G-d, when I shall be sanctified in you before their eyes. I shall take you from the nations, and I shall gather you from all the lands, and I shall bring you to your land. I shall sprinkle pure waters upon you and you shall be purified from all your sins, and I will purify you from all your idols.." (Ezekiel 36:22-25)

C. End to Evil and Sin

The Messianic era will mark the end of evil and sin:

Ezekiel 37:23: "They shall not defile themselves anymore with their idols and with their abominations and with all their transgressions.."

Zephaniah 3:13: "The remnant of Israel will not do any wrong, and they will not speak lies nor shall a deceitful tongue be found in their mouth."

Zechariah 13:2: "It shall be in that day .. that I shall cut off the names of the idols from the earth and they shall no longer be remembered; and I shall also remove from the earth the [false] prophets and the spirit of impurity."

Malachi 3:19: "For behold the day comes burning like a furnace, and all the wanton sinners and everyone that does wickedness shall be stubble .. that to them shall not be left root and branch."

Isaiah 60:21: "Your people shall all be righteous, they shall inherit the land forever.."

Jeremiah 50:20: "In those days and in that time, says G-d, the iniquity of Israel shall be searched for but it will not be, and the sins of Judah – but they shall not be found.."[10]

D. Awareness and Knowledge of G-d

The Messianic era will be a time of universal awareness, perception and knowledge of G-d:

Isaiah 11:9: *(cf.* Habakuk 2:14): "..the earth shall be full of knowledge of G-d as the waters cover the sea."

Isaiah 40:5: "The glory of G-d shall be revealed, and all flesh shall see together that the mouth of G-d has spoken."[10a]

---

10. For further details on the eradication of evil, the evil inclination and Satan, see *Sukah* 52a; *Eliyahu Rabba* ch. 4; *Bereishit Rabba* 48:11; *Pesikta Rabaty* 33:4; and *Yalkut Shimoni*, I:133, on Genesis 33:13, p. 42a.

10a. "In the present world, the *Shechinah* manifests Itself only to certain individuals [prophets]; in the time to come, however, 'the glory of G-d shall be revealed and all flesh shall see together..';" *Vayikra Rabba* 1:14. The Messianic era will thus witness an *empirical* manifestation of Divinity even as occurred with the revelation at Sinai; see *Tanchuma*, Bamidbar: end of par. 17; and *Tanya*, ch. 36. *Cf. Sha'ar Ha'emunah*, ch. 25; and see note following.

Isaiah 52:8: "..for eye to eye they shall see as G-d returns to Zion."

Jeremiah 31:32-33: "..I shall put My teaching in their inward parts and write it in their heart, and I shall be to them for G-d and they shall be to Me for a people. They shall no longer teach one another, and a man his brother, saying 'Know G-d,' for they shall all know Me – from the least of them to the greatest of them.."

The Divine spirit will be upon the people, endowing them with the power of prophecy and vision:

Joel 3:1-2: "..I shall pour out My spirit upon all flesh, and your sons and your daughters shall prophesy, your elders shall dream dreams, your young shall see visions. In those days I shall pour out My spirit also upon the servants and handmaids."[10b]

10b. "The Holy One, blessed is He, said: 'In the present world [only] certain individuals prophesied; in the world to come, however, all Israel will be made prophets, as it is said, 'It shall come to pass afterwards that I shall pour out My spirit upon all flesh, and your sons and your daughters shall prophesy..';'" *Tanchuma*, Beha'alotecha: end of par. 16. *Cf. Tikunei Zohar* 18:36b; and above, note 10a.

Note *Igeret Teyman*, end of ch. 3, that there will be a restoration of prophecy even before the actual manifestation of Mashiach. *Cf. Likkutei Sichot*, vol. II: Balak, p. 588*f.*

E. Universal Worship of G-d

Mashiach shall mend the whole world so that all shall serve G-d in unity:[11]

Zephaniah 3:9: "For then I shall turn to the peoples a pure tongue that all shall call upon the Name of G-d to serve Him with one consent."

Isaiah 2:2-3 and Michah 4:1-2: "..The mountain of G-d's House shall be established at the top of the mountains and it shall be raised above the hills, and all the nations shall stream to it. Many peoples shall go and say, 'Come, let us go up to the mountain of G-d, to the House of the G-d of Jacob, and let him [Mashiach] teach us of His ways and we shall go in His paths;' for from Zion shall go forth Torah, and the word of G-d from Jerusalem."[12]

Zechariah 9:16: "..every one that is left of all the nations that came against Jerusalem shall go up from year to year to bow before the King, G-d.."

Zechariah 14:9: "G-d shall be King over the entire earth. In that day G-d shall be One and His Name One."

F. Universal Peace and Harmony

The awareness and knowledge of G-d will remove the narrow-minded dispositions that lead to strife and war. It will be an era of peace and

---

11. *Hilchot Melachim* 11:4
12. See also Isaiah 60:14; and Zechariah 8:23.

harmony – in the Holy Land[13] and throughout the world:

Isaiah 2:4 and Michah 4:3: "..they shall beat their swords into plowshares and their spears into pruning-hooks. Nation shall not lift a sword against nation, nor shall they learn war any more." [Michah 4:4 continues: "Each man shall sit under his vine and under his fig-tree, and none shall make them afraid.."]

Hosea 2:20: "..I shall break from the earth the bow, the sword and warfare, and I shall make them lie down securely."

Zechariah 9:10: "..the bow of war shall be cut off, and [Mashiach] shall speak peace unto the nations.."

This new attitude of mankind will also be reflected in the animal world:

Isaiah 11:6-9: "The wolf shall dwell with the lamb and the leopard shall lie with the kid, and a calf with a lion's cub and a fatling together, and a small child shall lead them. The cow and the bear shall graze, their young ones shall lie down together, and the lion shall eat straw like cattle. An infant shall play over the hole of an asp, and the weaned child shall put out his hand over the eyeball of an adder. They will not harm or destroy on all My holy mountain, for the earth shall be full of the knowledge of G-d as the waters cover the sea."

Isaiah 65:25: "The wolf and the lamb shall feed together, and the lion shall eat straw like cattle, dust shall be the serpent's food. They shall

---

13. See Leviticus 25:18-19 and 26:5; Jeremiah 23:6 and 33:16; Ezekiel 28:26 and 34:25-28; Joel 4:17.

not harm nor destroy in all My holy mountain, says G-d."[14]

G. Resurrection of the Dead

"Your dead shall be revived, my corpses shall arise; awaken and sing you who dwell in the dust, for a dew of lights is your dew.." (Isaiah 26:19)

"Behold I will open your graves and raise you from your graves, My people; and I will bring you into the Land of Israel. You shall know that I am G-d when I open your graves and when I revive you from your graves, My people. I shall put My spirit into you and you will live, and I will place you upon your land, and you will know that I, G-d, have spoken and done, says G-d." (Ezekiel 37:12-14)

"Many of them that sleep in the land of dust shall awake.." (Daniel 12:2)[15]

---

14. See also Hosea 2:20
15. Resurrection of the Dead is another of the 13 fundamental Principles of the Faith (Rambam, Article 13), distinct from that of the Messianic redemption. It will occur after the redemption, the very last event of the Messianic era (see *Zohar* I:139a), thus in a way distinct from it. Even so, there are various stages in the process of resurrection itself, with some individuals rising before all others. Moses and Aaron, for example, will be present already in the very early period, when the *Bet Hamikdash* will be re-established, in order to guide the order and procedures of the Temple-service (see *Tossafot* on *Pesachim* 114b; and *cf. Devarim Rabba* 3:17 and similar passages). A number of other saints, too, will be revived at various stages prior to the

H. Blissful Utopia: End to Disease and Death

The Messianic era will witness ultimate physical and spiritual bliss. All will be healed.[16] The blind, the deaf and the dumb, the lame, whosoever has any blemish or disability, shall be healed from all their disabilities: "The eyes of the blind shall be clearsighted, and the ears of the deaf shall be opened.. the lame shall leap as a hart and the tongue of the dumb shall sing.." (Isaiah 35:5-6).[17] Death itself shall cease, as it is said, "Death shall be swallowed up forever and G-d shall wipe the tears from every face.." (Isaiah 25:8)[18]

---

general resurrection of the dead (see R. Joseph Albo, *Ikkarim* IV:35; R. David ibn Zimra, *Teshuvot Radvaz* III:no. 644; R. Daniel Tirani, *Ikrei Hadat (Ikrei Dinim)*, vol. II: Yoreh De'ah 36:66; *Sdei Chemed*, Kuntres Hakelalim, *s.v.* mem:klal 218; and the sources cited there).

For the whole subject of the resurrection, see especially *Sanhedrin* 90a-92b; *Pirkei deR. Eliezer* ch. 33-34; R. Saadiah Gaon, *Emunot Vede'ot*, sect. VII; Rambam, *Ma'amar Techiyat Hametim*; Ramban, *Sha'ar Hagemul*; R. Chasdai Crescas, *Or Hashem* III:4, ch. 1-4; and R. Menachem M. Schneerson *shalita*, *Teshuvot Ubi'urim*, ch. 8 and 11 (offering a comprehensive and systematic analysis of this subject).

16. *Bereishit Rabba* 20:5
17. *Bereishit Rabba* 95:1; *Tanchuma*, Vayigash:8 and Metzora:2 (and see ed. Buber, Vayigash:9 and Metzora:7).
18. *Pesachim* 68a; *Shemot Rabba* 30:2. See also *Midrash Tehilim* 145:1.

There will be a life of ease.[19] Our physical needs will be taken care of by others, as it is said, "Strangers shall stand and feed your flocks and aliens shall be your plowmen and your vinedressers." (Isaiah 61:5)[20]

The earth will manifest extraordinary fertility, yielding an overabundance of every kind of produce, and trees growing ripe fruits every day.[21] Zion's wilderness will be made "to be like Eden, and her desert like the garden of G-d" (Isaiah 51:3). "I will call for the grain and increase it .. and I will increase the fruit of the tree and the produce of the field.." (Ezekiel 36:29-30) ".. The plowman shall overtake the reaper, and the treader of grapes him who sows seed; and the mountains shall drip sweet wine, and all the hills shall melt." (Amos 9:13)[21*]

> "At that time there will be neither famine nor war, neither envy nor strife. All good things will be bestowed in abundance, and all delicacies will be accessible like dust."[22]

---

19. *Eliyahu Rabba* ch. 4.
20. See also Isaiah 49:23 and 60:10-12.
21. *Shabbat* 30b; *Ketuvot* 111b.
21*. *Cf.* Leviticus 26:5; and Joel 4:18, and see *Vayikra Rabba* 17:4, and *Pesikta deR. Kahana*, ch. VII, p. 65bf., and the notes there. See also Hosea 2:23f.

    Note that Amos 9:13 is one of the few Scriptural verses that contain all the letters of the *aleph-bet*. On the significance of this, see *Hadar Zekeinim*, R. Bachaya, and *Ba'al Haturim*, on Exodus 16·16; and R. Bachaya and *Ba'al Haturim* on Deuteronomy 4:34. *Cf.* below, note 99.
22. *Hilchot Melachim* 12:5. *Cf. Midrash Tehilim* 87:3 ("gold and silver will be like dust").

The wondrous events and conditions of the Messianic era will completely overshadow all and any miracles that happened before then, even those associated with the exodus from Egypt.[23]

---

23. Jeremiah 23:7-8; *Berachot* 12bf.

   Note that in Rambam's view the Messianic era will not see a setting aside of the laws of nature, but "the world will follow its normal course.. 'The only difference between the present world and the Messianic days is delivery from servitude to foreign powers' *(Berachot* 34b)." The prophecies of supernatural events and conditions are to be understood figuratively. *(Hilchot Melachim* 12:1-2; and *cf. Hilchot Teshuvah* 9:2) Even so, Rambam himself qualifies this view as a *personal* opinion and interpretation, allowing for the possibility that everything may be quite literal. *(Ma'amar Techiyat Hametim*, sect. 6. *Cf. Hilchot Melachim* 12:2 that no one is in a position to know the details of the events to occur until they have come to pass etc.)

   As noted by the commentaries on *Hilchot Melachim,* Rambam's view is fraught with many difficulties, as even he himself enumerates events and conditions (not the least of which would be the resurrection of the dead) which are clearly beyond the normal course of the laws of nature *(cf.* notes 22, 41, 51 and 68). One resolution to this problem is by distinguishing between two general periods in the Messianic era: a first stage following an essentially natural order, and a later stage marked by supranatural events and conditions. See R. Yitzchak Abarbanel, *Yeshu'ot Meshicho,* Iyun Hashlishi:ch. 7. For a comprehensive analysis of this subject, see *Likkutei Sichot,* Vol. XXVII, pp. 191-206. *Cf.* also *Or Hachayim* on Exodus 21:11 and Numbers 24:17!

Even so, these Divine blessings are not an end in themselves. They are but a *means* towards a higher goal:

> Our longing for the Messianic era is *not* for the sake of dominating the world, to rule over the heathens, or to be exalted by the nations. Nor is it that we might eat, drink and rejoice,[24] "have much produce and wealth, ride horses and indulge in wine and song, as thought by some confused people."[25]

It is, rather, to have relief from the powers that presently do not allow us to be preoccupied with Torah and *mitzvot* properly.[26] Our aspirations are to be free to devote ourselves to Torah and its wisdom, with no one to oppress and disturb us. We long for that time because there will be an assembly of the righteous, an era dominated by goodness, wisdom, knowledge and truth. It will be a time when the commandments of the Torah shall be observed without inertia, laziness or compulsion (other version: "worries, fear or compulsion").[27]

> The sole preoccupation of the whole world will be to know G-d. The Israelites will be great sages: they will know things that are presently concealed, and will achieve knowledge of their Creator to the utmost capacity of human beings, as it is

---

24. *Hilchot Melachim* 12:4
25. Rambam, *Perush HaMishnah*, Introduction to Sanhedrin ch. 10.
26. *Hilchot Teshuvah* 9:2
27. Sources cited in notes 24-26.

said, "The earth shall be full of the knowledge of G-d as the waters cover the sea." (Isaiah 11:9)[28]

---

28. *Hilchot Melachim* 12:5. *Cf. Netzach Yisrael*, ch. 42.

III. *Ikvot Meshicha:* The Time Immediately Before Mashiach

The time appointed by G-d for the Messianic redemption is a closely guarded secret.[29] Nonetheless, we are offered many hints to recognize its proximity: when certain conditions come about, await the imminent coming of Mashiach.

Most of these conditions are quite disturbing, clearly displaying a situation of the very "bottom of the pit."[30] One major source describes the world-condition in those days as follows: increase in insolence and impudence; oppressing

---

29. *Pesachim* 54b; *Midrash Tehilim* 9:2. See *Zohar Chadash,* Bereishit, 8a.
30. *Midrash Tehilim* 45:3. See *Ma'amarei Admur Hazaken-Ethalech,* p. 103*f.*; and *Besha'ah Shehikdimu-5672,* vol. I:p. 551; relating this to the principle (*Midrash Tehilim* 22:4; *Zohar* II:46a) that the darkest moments of the night are immediately before daybreak. *Cf. Zohar* I:170a. For this analogy see also the comment of R. Elijah, the Vilna Gaon, cited in *Even Shelemah,* ch. 11:5.

inflation; unbridled irresponsibility on the part of authorities; centers of learning will turn into bawdy houses; wars; many destitutes begging, with none to pity them; wisdom shall be putrid; the pious shall be despised; truth will be abandoned; the young will insult the old; family-breakup with mutual recriminations; impudent leadership.[31]

Other sources add: lack of scholars; succession of troubles and evil decrees; famines; mutual denunciations; epidemics of terrible diseases; poverty and scarcity; cursing and blaspheming; international confrontations – nations provoking and fighting each other.[32] In short, it will be a time of suffering that will make it look as if G-d were asleep. These are the birthpangs of Mashiach, bearable only in anticipation of the bliss that follows them.

> "When you see a generation ever dwindling, hope for him .. when you see a generation overwhelmed by many troubles as by a river, await him."[33] "When you see nations fighting each other, look toward the feet of Mashiach."[34]

Little wonder that some sages expressed apprehensions about those days in terms of, "Let [Mashiach] come, but let me not see him."[35] The prevailing attitude, however, is to await his coming in spite of all, even if thereafter we shall

---

31. *Sotah* 49b
32. *Sanhedrin* 97a; *Shir Rabba* 2:29.
33. *Sanhedrin* 98a
34. *Bereishit Rabba* 42:4. Note *Pesikta Rabaty* 37:2 (ed. Friedmann, ch. 36)!
35. *Sanhedrin* 98b

merit no more than sitting "in the shadow of his donkey's dung!"[36]

The troubles and agony of *chevlei Mashiach* (birthpangs of Mashiach), however, are not unavoidable:

> "What is man to do to be spared the pangs of Mashiach? Let him engage in Torah and acts of loving-kindness!"[37]

Moreover, there are also good and happy signs indicating the imminent coming of Mashiach: a good measure of prosperity;[38] a renewal of Torah-study;[39] and opening of the "gates of wisdom above and the wellsprings of wisdom below,"[40] evidenced also by scientific and technological discoveries and advances; a manifestation and propagation of the mystical teachings of the Torah;[41] and also – "In the time that Mashiach will awaken, many signs and miracles will occur in the world."[42]

---

36. *Ibid.* See also *Zohar* II:7aff.
37. *Sanhedrin* 98b
38. *Sanhedrin* 97a; *Shir Rabba* 2:29.
39. *Ibid.*
40. *Zohar* I:117a
41. *Zohar* I:118a. See *Zohar Chadash*, Tikunim, 96c; and *Mayanei Hayeshu'ah*, I:2. *Cf.* below, note 84. Note also *Igeret Teyman*, ch. 3, that prophecy shall be restored to Israel prior to the coming of Mashiach.
42. *Zohar* II:8a

IV. The Personality of Mashiach

A. Mashiach — Human

Mashiach and the Messianic age are the ultimate end for the world, preconceived from the very beginning, for which the world was created.[43] Mashiach, therefore, is one of the things that precede the creation.[44] This refers, however, to the principle and soul of Mashiach. On the actual level of the physical world's reality, Mashiach is a human being:

Mashiach is a human being, born in normal fashion of human parents.[45] The only qualification about his origins is that he is a

---

43. *Sanhedrin* 98b; *Pesikta Rabaty* 34:6 (ed. Friedmann, ch. 33). See also *Bereishit Rabba* 2:4; and *cf.* R. Bachaya on Genesis 1:2; and *Netzach Yisrael*, ch. 43.
44. *Pesachim* 54a; *Pirkei deR. Eliezer* ch. 3 (see there *Bi'ur Haradal* note 14); *Bereishit Rabba* 1:4 (and see there *Minchat Yehudah*). *Cf. Yeshu'ot Meshicho*, Iyun Hasheni:ch. 3.
45. *Or Hachamah* on *Zohar* II:7b; R. Chaim Vital, *Arba Me'ot Shekel Kessef,* ed. Tel Aviv 5724, p. 241a-b. See also *Yeshu'ot Meshicho*, Iyun Hashelishi:ch. 3*ff.*

descendant of King David,[46] through the lineage of his son Solomon.[47] From his birth onwards his righteousness will increase continually, and by virtue of his deeds he will merit sublime levels of spiritual perfection.[48]

B. Mashiach In Every Generation

Any time is a potential time for the coming of Mashiach.[49] This does not mean, however, that at the appropriate time he will suddenly emerge from Heaven to appear on earth.[50] On the contrary: Mashiach is already on earth, a human being of great saintly status (a *tzadik*) appearing and existing in every generation. "In every

---

46. See Isaiah 11:1; Jeremiah 23:5-6 and 33:14ff. See also II-Samuel 7:12-16, and Psalms 89. In this context, Mashiach is often referred to as (and identified with) David – see Hosea 3:5; Jeremiah 30:9; Ezekiel 34:23-24 and 37:24-25 *(cf.* below. note 51).
47. *Tanchuma*, Toldot:14, and in ed. Buber, par. 20 (and see there note 139); *Agadat Bereishit* ch. 44. (See *Emek Hamelech*, Hakdamah, ch. 12, p. 14d, and Sha'ar Kiryat Arba, ch. 112, p. 108d). Rambam, Principles, Article 12, and *Igeret Teyman*, ch. 3. *(Cf.* also his *Sefer Hamitzvot* II:262). *Cf. Zohar* I:110b and III:188a, and commentaries there.
48. Sources in note 45.
49. See below, ch. V.
50. A superficial glance at *Zohar* II:7b would seem to suggest this; but see the commentaries cited in note 45.

generation is born a progeny of Judah fit to be Israel's Mashiach!"[50*]

On the particular day that marks the end of the *galut*, when Mashiach will redeem Israel, the unique pre-existing soul of Mashiach – 'stored' in Gan Eden from aforetimes – will descend and be bestowed upon that *tzadik*.[51] R. Mosheh Sofer

---

50* R. Ovadiah of Bartenura, Commentary on Ruth (appended to *Mikra'ot Gedolot-Bamidbar*, p. 479), see there.

51. *Ibid*. Cf. *Igeret Teyman*, ch. 4: "With respect to his arising, he will not be known beforehand until it is declared to him .. a man, unknown prior to his manifestation, shall rise, and the signs and wonders that will come about through him will be the proof for the authenticity of his claim and pedigree.."

Note that this concept of the 'bestowal and infusion' of Mashiach's soul unto a living *tzadik* (related to the Kabbalistic concepts of *gilgul* and *ibbur* – reincarnation and 'impregnation') explains the identification of Mashiach with King David himself (see *Yeshu'ot Meshicho*, Iyun Harishon, ch. 5:hakdamah 6; and see also R. Ya'akov Emden's commentary on the hymns of Hoshana Rabba, end, *s.v.* hu David atzmo). Likewise, it explains the identification of Mashiach with Moses, when he is called "the first redeemer and the last redeemer" (see *Shemot Rabba* 2:4, and *Devarim Rabba* 9:9); and as noted in *Zohar* I:25b and 253a that the numerical equivalent of *Mosheh* is the same as that of *Shiloh* (the term in Genesis 49:10 denoting Mashiach): the soul of Mashiach is the "soul-of-the-soul" of Moses, so that in effect Moses will be the final redeemer (and there is no problem with the seeming discrepancy of Mashiach being a descendant of David of the tribe of Judah

summarizes this principle in his responsa:[52]

"As for the coming of the scion of David, I need to posit the following premise: Moses the first redeemer of Israel, reached the age of eighty years and did not know or sense that he would redeem Israel. Even when the Holy One, blessed be He, said to him, 'Come and I will send you to Pharao..' (Exodus 3:10), he declined and did not want to accept that mission. So it will be with the final redeemer.

> "The very day that the *Bet Hamikdash* was destroyed, was born one who, by virtue of his righteousness, is fit to be the redeemer.[53] At the proper time G-d will reveal Himself to him and send him, and then will dwell upon him the spirit of Mashiach which is hidden and concealed above until his coming.

"Thus we find also with Saul that the spirit of royalty and the Holy Spirit – which he had not sensed at all within himself – came upon him after he was anointed..

"The *tzadik* himself does not realize this potential. Because of our sins many such *tzadikim* passed away already. We did not merit

---

while Moses is a descendent of the tribe of Levi). See R. Chaim Vital's *Likutei Torah*, and *Sha'ar Hapesukim*, on Genesis 49:10. Note also *Or Hachayim* on Genesis 49:11!

52. Responsa *Chatam Sofer* VI:98. See also *Chatam Sofer al Hatorah*, ed. Stern, vol. II: p. 18a, on Exodus 4:26, and note 9 there.
53. See *Agadat Bereishit* ch. 67 (68). See also *Yerushalmi, Berachot* 2:4, and *Eichah Rabba* 1:51.

that the Messianic spirit was conferred upon them. They were fit and appropriate for this, but their generations were not fit.."[54]

C. The Character and Qualities of Mashiach:

"The spirit of G-d will rest upon him, a spirit of wisdom and understanding, a spirit of counsel and might, a spirit of knowledge and of the fear of G-d. He shall be inspired with fear of G-d, and he shall not judge with the sight of his eyes nor decide according to the hearing of his ears. He shall judge the poor with righteousness and decide with equity for

---

54. See also *Sdei Chemed*, Pe'at Hasadeh: Kelalim, *s.v.* aleph:sect. 70.

This explains why R. Akiva would consider Bar Kochba to be Mashiach (*Yerushalmi, Ta'anit* 4:5; see *Hilchot Melachim* 11:3; and *cf. Yeshu'ot Meshicho*, Iyun Harishon:ch.4). Furthermore, it explains a discussion in Sanhedrin 98b about the name of Mashiach, with different authorities suggesting Shiloh, Yinon, Chaninah and Menachem (*cf. Yeshu'ot Meshicho*, Iyun Hasheni, ch. 3, that the term *Mashiach* is an acronym of these four names): each school picked the name of its own master (Rashi). The implication is clear: each school regarded its own master as the most likely potential Mashiach of that generation by virtue of his saintliness and perfection; see R. Tzadok Hakohen, *Peri Tzadik*, Devarim:13. In later generations, too, we find the same attitude among the disciples of R. Isaac Luria, the Baal Shem Tov, the Vilna Gaon, R. Chaim David Azulay, and many other extraordinary personalities, as stated explicitly in their writings.

the humble of the earth; he shall smite the earth with the rod of his mouth and slay the wicked with the breath of his lips. Righteousness shall be the girdle of his loins, and faith the girdle of his reins." (Isaiah 11:2-5)[54*] "Through his knowledge My servant shall justify the righteous to the many.." (Isaiah 53:10)

"Behold, My servant shall be wise, he shall be exalted and lofty, and shall be very high." (Isaiah 52:13). His wisdom shall exceed even that of King Solomon;[55] he shall be greater than the patriarchs, greater than all the prophets after Moses, and in many respects even more exalted than Moses.[56] His stature and honor shall exceed that of all kings before him.[57] He will be an extraordinary prophet, second only to Moses,[58] with all the spiritual and mental qualities that are prerequisites to be endowed with the gift of prophecy.[59]

As a faithful shepherd he already cares so much about his people that he volunteered to suffer all kinds of agonies to assure that not a single Jew of all times will be lost.[60]

54*. See *Likkutei Diburim*, vol. II, p. 628*ff*.
55. *Hilchot Teshuvah* 9:2
56. *Tanchuma*, and *Agadat Bereishit*, cited above, note 47. *Cf. Yeshu'ot Meshicho*, Iyun Hashlishi:ch. 1. See also *Or Hatorah-Na"ch*, vol. I, p. 265*f*.
57. Rambam, Introduction to *Sanhedrin* X; Principles, Article 12 (in popular versions, though not in ed. Kapach); and *Igeret Teyman*, ch. 4.
58. *Hilchot Teshuvah* 9:2; *Igeret Teyman*, ch. 4.
59. See *Igeret Teyman*, ch. 4.
60. *Pesikta Rabaty* 37:1 (ed. Friedmann, ch. 36).

Mashiach shall meditate on the Torah[61] and be preoccupied with *mitzvot*. He shall teach all the Jewish people and instruct them in the way of G-d. He will prevail upon Israel to follow and observe the Torah, repair its breaches, and fight the battles of G-d.[62]

Mashiach will reveal altogether new insights, making manifest the hidden mysteries of the Torah,[63] to the point that "all the Torah learned in the present world will be vain compared to the Torah of Mashiach."[64]

Though Mashiach comes first and foremost to Israel, all the nations will recognize his wisdom

---

61. See *Midrash Tehilim* 2:9 and 110:4.
62. *Hilchot Teshuvah* 9:2; *Hilchot Melachim* 11:4. Note also *Yalkut Shimoni*, Pinchas:par. 776, that Mashiach will have the unique gift of understanding and persuading each individual despite the wide diversity in people's minds and attitudes.
63. *Eliyahu Zutta* ch. 20; *Oti'ot deR. Akiva, s.v.* zayin. See Rashi (and other commentaries) on Song 1:2. *Cf. Zohar* III:23a; and *Vayikra Rabba* 13:3. See also *Tanchuma*, ed. Buber, Chukat:24, and *Pesikta deR. Kahana*, ed. Buber, ch. IV (p. 39a*f.*), and the editor's notes there.
64. *Kohelet Rabba* 11:12. For a comprehensive analysis of the concept of the new manifestations of Torah in the Messianic era, discussing the various Halachic and philosophical issues involved, see R. Menachem M. Schneerson *shalita, Kuntres Be'inyan "Torah Chadashah Me'iti Tetze". Cf.* also the commentaries on *Zohar* III:23a; and R. Abraham Azulay, *Chessed Le'Avraham,* Mayan II: 11 and 27, and *ibid.* Mayan V:36.

and sublimity and submit to his rule.[65] He will guide and instruct them as well.[66]

There is no need for Mashiach to perform signs and wonders to prove himself.[67] Nonetheless, he will do so.[68]

---

65. *Midrash Tehilim* 2:3 and 87:6-7.
66. *Bereishit Rabba* 98:9 (see there *Minchat Yehudah*); *Midrash Tehilim* 21:1. *Cf.* above II-E.
67. *Hilchot Melachim* 11:2.
68. See *Midrash Pirkei Mashiach;* and end of *Perek R. Yoshiyahu.* Note *Or Hachayim* on Exodus 21:11; and *cf.* above, note 23.

V. Date of Mashiach's Coming

The actual date of the Messianic redemption is a guarded mystery unknown to man.[69] It will happen "in its time" (Isaiah 60:22), predetermined from the beginning of creation. This ultimate *ketz* (time for the 'end') is unconditional: it does not depend on Israel's merit, as it is said, "For My own sake, for My own sake, I will do it.." (Isaiah 48:11); "I wrought for My Name's sake that it should not be profaned in the eyes of the nations." (Ezekiel 20:9)[70]

Even so, the wording of Isaiah 60:22 seems to display a contradiction by stating "in its time *I will hasten it*": "in its time" means a set date; "I will hasten it" means that it may occur earlier, *before* "its time." The contradiction is resolved as follows: "If they are worthy – 'I will hasten it;' if not – 'in its time.' "[71]

The implication is clear: Mashiach can come *any* day, even before the predetermined date: *"This day* – if you will listen to His voice!"

---

69. See above, note 29.
70. *Zohar Chadash*, Tikunim, 95b. *Cf. Shemot Rabba* 25:12 (cited below, note 81).
71. *Sanhedrin* 98a. *Yerushalmi, Ta'anit* 1:1.

(Psalms 95:7)[72] Every generation has a special *ketz* of its own, for, as stated, Mashiach is alive and present in every generation, albeit concealed.[73] He is ready to be revealed at a moment's notice.[74] In the course of history prior to "its time" there are especially auspicious times when it is easier to effect his coming. To take

---

72. *Cf. Zohar Chadash,* Tikunim 95b, that every generation has its own special *ketz,* subject to Israel's merit *(cf. Even Shelemah* 11:9). Abarbanel notes that the history of the world is divisible into three periods of premature, contingent, and mature: the first stage is premature for the redemption; the second is one of continuous potential for the redemption, subject to Israel's merits; while the third and final stage is the one of the final *ketz,* the definite date of the actual redemption. *Yeshu'ot Meshicho,* Part I, p. 11b; and *ibid.,* Iyun Harishon, ch. 1, end of p. 18b. *Cf. Sanhedrin* 97b, "Before that do not expect him; afterwards you may await him;" and *cf.* below, note 122. This serves also as one explanation why the redemption did not yet occur, in spite of the infinitely greater piety and saintliness of our ancestors; see Chida, *Petach Einayim* on *Sanhedrin* 98a; and below, ch. VIII.
73. See above, ch. IV-B.
74. See *Sanhedrin* 98a "he unties and rebandages each bandage separately, saying, 'Should I be wanted, I must not be delayed;'" Rashi: he does not treat two sores together, thinking 'if I need to go and redeem Israel, I will not delay because of bandaging two sores.'

advantage of these, to hasten the redemption, that depends completely on us.[75]

---

75. This may explain why many sages calculated specific dates for the Messianic redemption. They did so in spite of the Talmudic disapproval of such practice lest disillusionment lead to despair: people may say, "since the calculated time has arrived but Mashiach has not come, he will never come." *(Sanhedrin* 97b; and see *Or Hatorah-Na"ch*, vol. I, p. 183*f.*) Yet those who calculated dates for the *ketz* included the greatest sages and saints throughout the ages, like R. Saadiah Gaon, Rashi, Ba'alei Tossafot, Ramban, Abarbanel, R. Isaac Luria etc. (see *Mayanei Hayeshu'ah* I:ch. 1-2; and R. Reuven Margolius' glosses on *Teshuvot Min Hashamayim*, sect. 72, pp. 80-83). Rambam, after citing the Talmudic injunction in his code and elaborating on it in his *Igeret Teyman*, himself offers in the latter (ch. 3) a date passed on to him by his ancestors! Ramban confronts the problem by stating that the Talmudic prohibition was but for a limited time only and no longer applies to the present era of *ikvot Meshicha*. (See his *Sefer Hage'ulah*, ed. Chavel, p. 289*f.*, and see there also pp. 262 and 263). *Cf.* below, note 122. Various sources explain that all these were in fact true predictions, reflecting especially auspicious times. Mystics state that these dates were in fact actualized, though so far, unfortunately, only in spiritual dimensions not perceived on the manifest level of our reality. *(Kuntres Perush Hamilot*, ch. 27 (p. 15b). See also *Maamarei Admur Hazaken – Haketzarim*, p. 212; *Bnei Yisas'char*, Sivan V:19; *Ateret Tzvi* on *Zohar* II:10a. *Cf. Bet Elokim*, Sha'ar Hatefilah, ch. 17.)

VI. Hastening the Coming of Mashiach

There are a number of ways conducive to hasten the Messianic redemption prior to its final date. Generally speaking these involve the observance of some special *mitzvot* which constitute comprehensive principles of the Torah.

A. Special *Mitzvot*

Teshuvah: First and foremost among these *mitzvot* is the principle of *teshuvah*. "When you return unto G-d, your G-d, and will listen to His voice.. G-d, your G-d, will return your captivity and have compassion upon you, and He will restore and gather you from all the nations to which G-d, your G-d, has dispersed you.." (Deuteronomy 30:2ff.) *Teshuvah* will bring about an immediate redemption, *"Today,* if you will listen to His voice." (Psalms 95:7)[76]

---

76. *Sanhedrin* 98a; *Zohar Chadash*, Bereishit, 8a. *Hilchot Teshuvah* 7:5. See *Midrash Hagadol* on Deuteronomy 30:2; and below, note 78.

"Watchman (i.e., G-d), what will be of the night (i.e., the *galut*)? Said the Watchman: 'Morning (i.e., the redemption) has come, and also night (i.e., retribution for the heathens and oppressors of Israel); if you will request, request. Return and come!'" (Isaiah 21:11-12) G-d says that *He* is ready, indeed anxious, to make the 'morning' shine for us. Upon Israel's question 'when?,' the Divine response is: "Whenever *you* want, He wants! If you want to make your request to hasten the end, request!" What then is deterring the redemption? The lack of *teshuvah;* thus "Return and come!"[77]

Teshuvah, the comprehensive principle of submission to G-d and His will, thus is the most obvious means to bring about the immediate coming of Mashiach.[78] It does not require any extraordinary action or undertaking: the simple – though sincere – thought of regretting misdeeds with determination to better our ways is already complete *teshuvah.*[79]

Shabbat: If Israel will keep just one Shabbat properly, Mashiach will come immediately.[80] "Though I have set a limit to 'the end,' that it will happen in its time regardless of whether they will do *teshuvah* or not .. the scion of David

---

77. *Yerushalmi, Ta'anit* 1:1, cited by Rashi and Redak on Isaiah 21:11-12. See also *Zohar Chadash,* Bereishit 8a.
78. See *Sanhedrin* 97bf; *Yerushalmi, Ta'anit* 1:1; and *Zohar Chadash,* Noach 23c-d.
79. *Pesikta Rabaty* 45:9 (ed. Friedmann, ch. 44); *Kidushin* 49b. See *Zohar* I:129a-b; and *cf. Avodah Zara* 17a. Note the trenchant comments of Chafetz Chaim on the application of the condition of *teshuvah* to the present time, in *Tzipita Liyeshu'ah,* ch. 1.
80. *Yerushalmi, Ta'anit* 1:1

(Mashiach) will come if they keep just one Shabbat, because the Shabbat is equivalent to all the *mitzvot*."[81]

Torah-study: "Torah-study is equivalent to all [the *mitzvot*]." (Pe'ah 1:1) By virtue of Torah they will return to the Holy Land and be gathered in from the exile.[82] Israel shall be redeemed by virtue of ten people sitting one with the other, each of them studying with the other.[83]

Especially significant in this context is the study of *pnimiyut Hatorah,* the mystical dimension of the Torah: "In the merit thereof 'You shall proclaim liberty throughout the land' (Leviticus 25:10)."[84]

Tzedakah, too, is equivalent to all the *mitzvot.*[85] Our compassion for the needy and downcast evokes a reciprocal compassion from Heaven, thus hastening the day of the scion of David (Mashiach) and the days of our redemption.[86] "Zion shall be redeemed by justice and her repatriates by *tzedakah.*" (Isaiah 1:27) "Keep justice and do *tzedakah,* for My salvation

---

81. *Shemot Rabba* 25:12
82. *Zohar* III:270a. See there also 178b.
83. *Eliyahu Zutta,* end of ch. 14 (see there *Yeshu'ot Ya'akov,* note 4).
84. *Tikunei Zohar* 6:23bf. See also *Zohar* III:124b; *Tikunei Zohar* 31:53b; *Zohar Chadash,* Tikunim 96c; and the sources cited in my *The Mystical Tradition,* p. 115ff; and see *Even Shelemah* 11:3, and *ibid.,* note 5 (end of p. 52a).
85. *Baba Batra* 9a
86. *Eliyahu Zutta,* ch. 1. See *Shabbat* 139a; Rambam, *Hilchot Matnot Aniyim* 10:1.

is near to come and My *tzedakah* to be revealed." (Isaiah 56:1)[87]

Other *mitzvot* charged with special efficacy to bring about the redemption are procreation (Genesis 1:28),[88] the four species of Sukot (Leviticus 23:40),[89] and the sending away of the mother-bird (Deuteronomy 22:6-7).[90]

B. Unity of Israel

Before Jacob passed away, he addressed all his sons: *"Gather together* and I shall tell you that which shall occur to you in the end of days. *Assemble yourselves* and hear.." (Genesis 49:1-2) With these words he warned them against any dissension among themselves.[91] He said to them:

> "Though it is not known when the Day of Judgment will be, I do tell you that the hour you gather and assemble together you shall be redeemed, as it is said, 'I will surely gather Jacob, all of you [i.e., when all of you are together]..' – for then immediately – 'their king shall pass before

---

87. See *Baba Batra* 10a. – See also below, note 117, for another sense of *tzedakah* by virtue of which we shall be redeemed.
88. *Eliyahu Zutta*, ch. 14. See *Yevamot* 62a.
89. *Bereishit Rabba* 63:8; *Vayikra Rabba* 30:16.
90. *Devarim Rabba* 6:7. See *Tikunei Zohar* 6:23a-b; and see *Keter Shem Tov*, sect. 415.
91. *Bereishit Rabba* 98:2. See *Midrash Hagadol* on Genesis 49:1; and *cf. Sifre*, Berachah, par. 346.

them and G-d at the head of them.' (Michah 2:12-13)."[92]

The unity of Israel, all being as one, is the preparation and condition for the ultimate redemption.[93]

> "It is presently 'dark' for you, but the Holy One, blessed be He, will in the future illuminate for you as an everlasting light, as it is said, 'G-d shall be for you an everlasting light' (Isaiah 60:19). When will that be? When all of you will be a singular band.. Israel will be redeemed when they shall be a singular band, as it is said, 'In those days and in that time, says G-d, the children of Israel shall come, they and the children of Judah *together..*' (Jeremiah 50:4); and it is said, 'In those days, the house of Judah shall walk with the house of Israel, and they shall *come together* from the land of the north to the land I have given as a legacy to your fathers' (Jeremiah 3:18). When they are bound together they shall receive the Face of the Shechinah!"[94]

Internal unity, *ahavat Yisrael,* peace and harmony, safeguard even against punishment for the worst sin;[95] but when "their heart is divided, they shall bear their guilt." (Hosea 10:2)[96]

---

92. *Agadat Bereishit,* ch. 82 (83).
93. *Bereishit Rabba* 98:2.
94. *Tanchuma,* Nitzavim:1.
95. See *Tanchuma,* Tzav:6 and Shoftim:18; *Bereishit Rabba* 38:6; and see also *Devarim Rabba* 5:10.
96. *Bereishit Rabba* 38:6

Notwithstanding the idyllic *ritual* observance in the days of the Second Temple, dissension, gratuitous hatred and divisiveness, caused the destruction of the *Bet Hamikdash* and the present *galut*.[97] Rectification of this condition will bring about the restoration of the *Bet Hamikdash* and the Messianic redemption.[98]

One other principle to hasten and actualize the Messianic redemption, of utmost significance and in fact at the very core of our affirmation of the fundamental doctrine of Mashiach, is the very belief in, and anticipation of, the coming of Mashiach:

---

97. *Yoma* 9b; and see also *Tossefta, Menachot* 13:22.
98. See my *Chassidic Dimensions*, pp. 64-67, 78f., and 188, and the sources cited there. *Cf. Keter Shem Tov*, sect. 370; and R. Dov Ber of Mezhirech, *Maggid Devarav Leya'akov*, sect. 235.

VII. Awaiting Mashiach

A. The Obligation to Await

"The vision is yet for an appointed time, but at the end it shall speak and not lie. Though he tarry – *wait for him,* for it will surely come.. it will not be late!" (Habakuk 2:3)

"Therefore *wait for Me,* says G-d, for the day that I rise to the prey; for My judgment is to gather nations, that I assemble kingdoms, to pour out upon them My indignation, all My fierce anger. For all the earth shall be consumed by the fire of My jealousy." (Zephaniah 3:8)[99]

---

99. Note that this is another of the few Scriptural verses that contain all the letters of the *aleph-bet* (see above, note 21*). As noted by various texts, however, it is the *only* one which also contains the final forms of the five letters *(mem, nun, tzadik, peh, kaf)* which have double forms. The additional significance of this follows from the fact that these five letters "all pertain to the mystery of the redemption!" *Pirkei deR. Eliezer,* ch. 48 *(cf. Aruch, s.v.* chamesh; and note R. Bachaya

"Happy are all those that wait for him." (Isaiah 30:18)[100]

Waiting for Mashiach, anticipating his coming, is not simply a virtue but a religious obligation. Rambam thus rules that whoever does not believe in – and whoever does not *await (eagerly looking forward to)* – the coming of Mashiach, in effect denies the whole Torah, all the prophets beginning with Moses.[101] In the popular formulation of his thirteen Principles of the Faith (the hymn of *Ani Ma'amin*) this is put as follows:

> *"I believe with complete faith in the coming of Mashiach. Though he tarry, nonetheless I await him every day, that he will come."*

As stated above,[102] some authorities view this principle as an integral part of the first of the Ten Commandments which states *"Anochi* – I am G-d, your G-d, who has taken you out of the land of Egypt, out of the house of bondage." (Exodus 20:2) The connection may be seen in the fact

---

on Genesis 47:28, and Redak on Isaiah 9:6). *Cf.* also *Bamidbar Rabba* 18:21, and parallel passages.

100. See *Sanhedrin* 97b. *Cf.* also Rashi on Isaiah 26:2 and Psalms 130:6.
101. See above, note 3. For a comprehensive analysis of Rambam's ruling, see *Chidushim Ubi'urim Behilchot Melachim*, sect. II.
102. See above, note 4.

that the initial word – *Anochi* – is linked with redemption:

"*Anochi* signifies the first redemption from Egypt and the last redemption through Mashiach."[103] *Anochi* is an explicit expression of compassion, consolation and comfort.[104] Indeed, *Anochi* is an acronym with every one of its four letters signifying Biblical prophecies of the Messianic consolations and comfort.[105]

In view of this legal obligation to await Mashiach, therefore, one of the first questions an individual is asked on the Day of Divine Judgment is *"Tzipita liyeshu'ah* – did you look forward to salvation?"[106]

To believe in the coming of Mashiach and to await it are two separate concepts. "To believe" is a doctrinal affirmation as for any other part of the Torah: affirming the principle of Mashiach who will come eventually, whenever that may be. "To await" means an active and eager anticipation of the redemption, that it occur speedily: *"I await him every day..,"* literally:[107]

---

103. *Shemot Rabba* 3:4. See *Mayim Rabim-5636*, ch. 134 (p. 144f.).
104. *Pesikta Rabaty* 21:15. See there also 34:8 (ed. Friedmann, ch. 33, p. 153a). *Cf. Torah Shelemah,* Yitro, on Exodus 20:2, notes 33, 34, and 46.
105. See *Midrash Hagadol* on Deuteronomy 5:6 (p. 103).
106. *Shabbat* 31a
107. See *Zohar* I:4a: "Who among you awaits *every day* the light that will shine forth.. [i.e., "awaiting the coming of Mashiach every day;" Commentary of R. Abraham Galante, cited there in *Or Hachamah*] when [the King] shall be glorified and called King over all the kings in the world? He who does not look forward to

"In *ikveta deMeshicha* (on the 'heels of Mashiach,' i.e.,) when the time arrives for the glory of G-d to be revealed in the world through the coming of our righteous Mashiach, there will surely be leaders of Israel .. who will urge the masses of Israel to strengthen the faith and to return with *teshuvah,* and to arouse the people to prepare themselves with *teshuvah* and good deeds for the coming of Mashiach..

"In those days there will also be people of little faith who will not believe those words, even as we find that during the Egyptian exile 'they did not listen to Moses because of anguished spirit and hard labor' (Exodus 6:9)..

"Each one will argue that he does not question the truth of the possibility of the redemption, but merely doubts the time of the redemption as to when it will occur. Yet there is an explicit verse in Malachi (3:1) that 'The lord whom you seek (i.e., the king Mashiach) will *suddenly* come to his palace, and the messenger

---

this *every day* [i.e., he does not await the salvations *every day; ibid.*] in this world, has no share here." ["This is the concept of 'Did you look forward to salvation?'. That is why (the sages) instituted to say in the 'Eighteen Blessings' *(Amidah;* 15th Blessing) 'for we hope for Your salvation every day (lit. all the day);'" Commentary of R. Chaim Vital, cited there in *Or Hachamah. Cf. Peri Eitz Chayim,* Sha'ar Ha'amidah ch. 19: when saying "for we hope for Your salvation all the day," have in mind that man is asked after death, "Did you look forward to salvation?"] See also *Zohar* I:140a: "..those that eagerly await the redemption each day, as it is said, 'A hoard of salvation' (Isaiah 33:6) – which refers to those who eagerly await salvation every day."

of the covenant whom you desire (i.e., Elijah the prophet), behold he comes..' At the very least, therefore, one is to consider every day that perhaps he will come that day. We find this reflected in the explicit ruling in the *Gemara*[108] about one who vows to become a nazirite on the day that the scion of David will come..

"[If one does not sense it this way] it follows that the belief in the coming of Mashiach is extremely weak. All our talk about our righteous Mashiach is but outwardly, while our heart is not with us.."[109]

B. *Kivuy:* The Merit and Effect of Awaiting

"Everything is (bound up) with *kivuy* (hoping; awaiting)."[110]

"When Israel asked Bil'am, 'When will salvation come?' he answered them: 'I see him, but not now; I behold him, but not nigh'

---

108. *Eruvin* 43a-b. See *Radvaz* on Rambam, *Hilchot Nezirut* 4:11.
109. Chafetz Chaim, *Chizuk Emunah*, quoted in *Chafetz Chaim al Hatorah*, Vayera, p. 56f., note 2. Note also *Torat Ze'ev*, quoted in *Hagadah shel Pesach Mibet Levi* [*Brisk*], p. 120: "It is incumbent to await the coming of Mashiach every single day, and all day long.. It is not enough to believe in the coming of Mashiach, but each day one must await his coming.. Furthermore, it is not enough to await his coming every day, but it is to be in the manner of our prayer 'we await Your salvation all the day,' that is, to await and expect it *every* day, and *all day long*, literally every moment!"
110. *Bereishit Rabba* 98:14

(Numbers 24:17). Said the Holy One, blessed be He, to them: 'Is this your sense? Do you not know that Bil'am .. does not wish My salvation to come? Be like your patriarch who said, 'I wait for Your salvation, G-d' (Genesis 49:18).[111] Wait for salvation for it is close at hand!' Thus it says, 'For My salvation is near to come' (Isaiah 56:1)."[112]

"When the Israelites enter the synagogues and houses of study, they say to the Holy One, blessed be He, 'Redeem us!' He responds to them: 'Are there righteous people among you? Are there G-d-fearing people among you?' They reply: 'In the past .. there were.. Nowadays, however, as we go from generation to generation it grows darker for us..' The Holy One, blessed be He, then says to them: 'Trust in My Name and I shall stand by you .. for I shall save whoever trusts in My Name.'"[113]

"Israel has nothing but the hope that the Holy One, blessed be He, redeem them by virtue of 'I hoped patiently unto G-d' (Psalms 40:2), as it is written, 'G-d is good unto those that hope unto Him' (Lament. 3:25). If you might say, 'The harvest is past, the summer is ended, and we are not saved' (Jeremiah 8:20), then 'Hope to G-d, be strong and let your heart take courage, and hope to G-d' (Psalms 27:14) .. hope and hope again. If you should ask, 'Until when should we hope?' – it was already said, 'Let Israel hope to G-d, from this time and forever' (Psalms 131:3), and 'Be strong and let your heart take courage, all those that hope to G-d' (Psalms 31:25). If this will be

---

111. See *Targum Yehonathan*, and *Bereishit Rabba* 98:14, on this verse.
112. *Shemot Rabba* 30:24
113. *Midrash Tehilim* 31:1

done, you shall be saved, as it is said, 'Those that hope in Me will not be ashamed' (Isaiah 49:23), 'Those that hope to G-d shall renew their strength' (Isaiah 40:31), and 'Those that hope to G-d shall inherit the land' (Psalms 37:9)."[114]

Though the study of Torah is ever so important, the need to await and hope for the redemption is addressed especially to the scholars and students of Torah, as G-d rebukes them: "Though the words of the Torah are beloved unto you, you did not do right in awaiting My Torah but not (the restoration of) My Kingdom."[115]

> "[The patriarchs] exclaimed before Him: 'Master of the universe, maybe there is no restoration for the children?' He said to them: 'When there is a generation that looks forward to My Kingdom, they will be redeemed immediately,' as it is said, 'There is hope for your future, says G-d, that (your) children shall return to their own boundary' (Jeremiah 31:16)."[116]

The daily *Amidah* contains the request, "Speedily cause the offspring of Your servant David to flourish and enhance his power through Your salvation, for we hope for Your salvation all the day.." The last phrase, "for we hope..," seems strange: what kind of reasoning is that? If we justly deserve the redemption, we shall merit it even without that hope; if we do

---

114. *Midrash Tehilim* 40:1
115. *Pesikta Rabaty* 35:2 (ed. Friedmann, ch. 34).
116. *Eychah Zutta*, par. 26 (ed. Buber, p. 65); *Yalkut Shimoni* II:997.

not deserve it, of what avail will that hope be? The meaning, however, is clear:

> "Speedily cause the offspring of Your servant David to flourish..;" and if it should be said that we lack merit, cause it to flourish anyway – *"because* we hope for your salvation..," that is, because we have the *kivuy* (hope). By virtue of that *kivuy* we *deserve* that You redeem us!117

C. Demanding Mashiach

True belief in the Messianic redemption is reflected and verified in sincere anticipation, in eagerly looking forward to the coming of Mashiach. In turn, the sincerity of this hope and awaiting is tested by what is done to achieve it.

---

117. *Tzemach David,* quoted in *Midbar Kedemot, s.v.* kivuy (kof: par. 16). – In this context note also *Tossafot Harosh* on Genesis 15:6: "He believed in G-d, and He accounted it to him as *tzedakah,"* i.e., the Holy One, blessed be He, accounted to Abraham the faith he had in Him as *tzedakah* (lit. meritorious righteousness). This shows that the prophet's words that "Zion shall be redeemed by justice and her repatriates by *tzedakah"* (Isaiah 1:27) .. and many other such verses, do not refer only to one's personal or monetary *tzedakah* (charity). The complete faith of Israel believing all the promises given unto them through the prophets is also referred to as *tzedakah*. It is worthy in the eyes of G-d, and (by virtue thereof) in His great compassion He will bring upon us that which He promised us. *Cf. Mechilta,* Beshalach, Vayehi: end of ch. 6; *Eliyahu Rabba,* ch. 25; and Maharal, *Netzach Yisrael,* ch. 26.

For something truly desired one will ask and beg, demand, and do everything possible to attain it. The same applies to the obligatory awaiting and anticipation of Mashiach.

G-d insists that we prove the sincerity of our claim to want Mashiach by doing everything in our power to bring it about, including storming the Gates of Heaven with demands for the redemption:

> "The children of Israel shall sit many days without king and without prince, and without sacrifice.. Thereafter, the children of Israel shall return and *ask* for G-d, their G-d, and for David their king, and they shall be in fear before G-d and (hope) for His goodness in the end of days." (Hosea 3:4-5)

"Ask for G-d" refers to the restoration of the Kingdom of Heaven; "David their king" – the restoration of the Kingdom of the House of David, through Mashiach; "fear before G-d.. His goodness" – the restoration of the *Bet Hamikdash*. For Israel will not see the redemption until they shall return and *ask* for these![118]

"Israel shall not be redeemed until they will confess and *demand* the Kingdom of Heaven, the Kingdom of the House of David, and the *Bet Hamikdash!*"[119]

---

118. *Midrash Shemuel*, ch. 13, cited by Rashi and Redak on Hosea 3:4-5.
119. *Bet Yossef* on *Tur-Orach Chayim* ch. 188 (from the Midrash cited above, as quoted by *Shibalei Haleket*, sect. 157).

R. Shimon bar Yochai taught a parable of a man who punished his son. The son did not know why he was being punished, but thereafter his father said to him: "Now go and do that which I had ordered you many days ago and you ignored me."

"Even so, all the thousands that perished in battle in the days of David, perished only because they did not demand that the *Bet Hamikdash* be built. This presents an *a fortiori* argument:

> "If this happened to those in whose midst there had not been a *Bet Hamikdash*, which, therefore, was not destroyed in their days, yet they were punished *for not demanding it,* how much more so then with regards to ourselves in whose days the *Bet Hamikdash* is destroyed and we do not mourn it and do not seek mercy for it!"[120]

We pray for the redemption several times every day. Even so, requesting by itself is not enough. One *must demand* the redemption, just as with the wages of a hired worker: the law stipulates that if the worker does not *demand* his wages, there is no obligation to give it to him on the very day that he completes his work.[121] So, too, we must *demand* our redemption. Failure to

---

120. *Midrash Tehilim* 17:4; *Midrash Shemuel*, ch. 31; cited by Redak on II-Samuel 24:25, see there; and in Halachic context in *Roke'ach*, Hilchot Tefilah, sect. 322. See also Responsa *Chatam Sofer* VI:no. 86.
121. *Baba Metzia* 9:12 (111a)

do so shows that this matter is clearly not that urgent to us![122]

---

122. *Sichot Chafetz Chaim*, par. 14; quoted in *Chafetz Chaim al Siddur Hatefilah*, par. 168 (p. 80).

Note in this context that *Yerushalmi, Ta'anit* 1:1 enumerates as one of the five things by virtue of which Israel shall be redeemed, *"tzevachah* – an outcry of prayer" for the redemption (*cf.* the version in *Midrash Tehilim* 106:9).

As for *Ketuvot* 111a and *Shir Rabba* 2:7 (*cf. Tanchuma*, ed. Buber, Devarim:4, note 13) that G-d adjured Israel not to press for a hastening of the *ketz (cf.* Rashi on *Ketuvot* 111a, "through excessive prayer"): (a) Note Responsa *Avnei Nezer*, Yoreh De'ah, no. 454, par. 40*ff.*, that this does not fall into Halachic purview of practical implications. (b) The adjuration to Israel was counterbalanced by another one to the nations of the world not to make the yoke of exile too heavy on Israel "for by making their yoke too heavy on Israel they would cause the end to come before its time!" (*Shir Rabba, ibid.*) As the nations clearly violated the oath addressed to them, therefore, Israel is freed from its own. (*Cf.* Maharal, *Netzach Yisrael*, ch. 24; and see *Kovetz Torah shebe'al Peh*, vol. XIII, Jerusalem 1971, pp. 144-5.)

Moreover, (c) *Berayta deR. Yishmael* in *Pirkei Heichalot* (cited in R. Chaim Vital's introduction to *Eitz Chayim*) states – in comment on Daniel 7:25 – that these adjurations were in effect for 1000 years only, and no more! (*Cf. Zohar* II:17a; and also *ibid.*, I:116b). *Cf.* Chida, *Midbar Kedemot, s.v.* gimel:25, and *Devash Lefi, s.v.* yod:11 (which seems based on R. Chaim Vital's *Sha'ar Hapesukim*, Daniel 12); and see also *Petach Einayim* on *Sanhedrin* 98a.

On the issue of Messianic activism, see also *Darkei Chayim Veshalom (Munkatsh)*, pp. 143*ff.* and 213*ff.*

VIII. Now – More Than Ever!

It is fair to ask why the present generation should be able to merit the Messianic redemption when this was withheld from our predecessors. It would seem rather presumptuous on our part when those before us were ever so much greater and more pious than we are: "If the earlier generations were like angels, we are but like plain humans; if they were like humans, we are like donkeys..!"[123]

In fact, however, this is not really a problem. For one thing, there is an obvious progression of time which of itself brings us closer to Mashiach and continuously enhances the inherent potential for redemption, in spite of our inferiority.[124]

Secondly, the very deterioration of our times and conditions, making it so much more difficult to achieve spiritual perfection, lends that much more value and merit to even our slightest virtues, for "one thing in distress is better than a

---

123. *Yerushalmi, Shekalim* 5:1; *Shabbat* 112b. See also *Eruvin* 53a; *Yoma* 9b; and *Zohar* III:2a.
124. See *Petach Einayim* on *Sanhedrin* 98a.

hundred in ease."[125] Greatness does not depend simply on the quantitative achievements of man, but is relative to the time and conditions of the generation: "a very small act in this generation is equal to many great *mitzvot* in others; for in these generations evil is extremely overpowering, to no end, unlike aforetimes!"[126]

Moreover, evil in itself has no reality. It is merely a state of concealment and hiding of the good.[127] Goodness and virtue, on the other hand, are realities with the quality of permanence. They do not fade away.[128] All the *mitzvot* and good deeds of the past, our own and those of our predecessors, therefore, remain intact. Thus there is an ever-growing accumulative merit accruing to our credit. Our present generation compounds not only its own goodness and merits but also those of all earlier generations.[129] In the words of an ancient proverb,[130] we are *"like a midget standing on the shoulders of a giant":* though the midget is much smaller than the giant, by virtue of standing on his shoulders, he can see much further. That is why it is

---

125. *Avot deR. Nathan* 3:6. *Cf. Shir Rabba* 8:10.
126. R. Chaim Vital, *Sha'ar Hagilgulim*, ch. 38, see there at length. *Cf. Hilchot Teshuvah* 3:2.
127. See *Netzach Yisrael*, ch. 31. *Cf. Moreh Nevuchim* III:10-12. *Tzava'at Harivash*, ch. 130, and the notes there.
128. *Cf. Sha'ar Hagilgulim*, ch. 3-4.
129. *Cf. Yerushalmi, Ta'anit* 1:1, and *Midrash Tehilim* 106:9 (cited above, note 122), that *zechut avot* (merit of the ancestors) is one of the five things by virtue of which Israel shall be redeemed.
130. Cited in author's foreword of *Shibalei Haleket*, see there.

specifically *now* – more than ever before – that we shall merit the coming of Mashiach.

> *"Therefore we put our hope to You, G-d, our G-d, that we may speedily see the splendor of Your might.. to perfect the world through the sovereignty of the Almighty. Then all mankind will invoke Your Name .. and accept upon themselves the yoke of Your Kingship.. On that day G-d shall be One and His Name One."*[131]

---

131. *Aleinu*-Prayer. – It would seem that there remains a problem with regards to the obligation to await, anticipate or look forward with eagerness to the imminent coming of Mashiach, and of persistent prayer or demand for the Messianic redemption. This obligation is clearly premised on personal *feelings*, on *sensing* the intrinsic need and benefits of the redemption, notwithstanding the fact that feelings cannot be legislated. How, then, can there be such an obligation, let alone the principle that "everything is bound up with *kivuy*"?

    The same question, however, applies no less to other religious duties that involve human sentiments, especially the fundamental *mitzvot* of loving and fearing G-d. The answer in that context, therefore, applies equally to the one about Mashiach: "What is the way that will lead to the love of [G-d] and the fear of Him? When a person contemplates His great and wondrous works and creatures and perceives from them His wisdom which is beyond comparison and limit, he will immediately love Him, praise Him, glorify Him, and long with an exceeding longing to know His great Name.. When pondering these very subjects, he will recoil in fear and dread, realizing that he is but a small creature, lowly and obscure, with slight and slender intelligence, standing in the presence of Him who is perfect in knowledge.." (Rambam, *Hilchot Yessodei Hatorah* 2:2; see there also 4:12; *Hilchot Teshuvah* 10:6; and note especially his *Sefer Hamitzvot*, Positive Precepts, no. 3.)

So, too, with regards to Mashiach and the redemption: pondering that this is a fundamental doctrine of the Divine Torah, studying and understanding the meaning of the laws and concepts of Mashiach, redemption, the Messianic era and all that is related to these (see especially *Hilchot Melachim* ch. 11-12, and the sources cited above), must of itself evoke the appropriate appreciation and longing for these.

In the same context, one is to consider also Rambam's ruling that man can train himself to acquire proper dispositions by frequent repetition of actions consistent with these, "and thus these dispositions will become a fixed part of his soul." (*Hilchot De'ot* 1:7; see his *Shemonah Perakim*, ch. 4. Cf. *Zohar* III:92b, and also *ibid.* 34b and 119a.) Diligent study of the *halachot* and ideas relating to Mashiach will thus result in the proper dispositions and sentiments, even if at first they are not sensed on a natural level. (See the essay, "Serve G-d With Joy," in my *Chassidic Dimensions*, especially p. 145f., and the sources cited there.) This, in turn, shall no doubt result immediately in the Divine response of redeeming Israel and the full realization of all the prophecies about the Messianic era.

SUPPLEMENTS

Supplements

R. Mosheh ben Maimon (Rambam), *Mishneh Torah:*
Hilchot Melachim, chapters 11-12 73

Appendix I:
   The Prophet Elijah – Harbinger of the
   Redemption 89

Appendix II:
   Mashiach ben Yossef 93

Bibliography 103

MISHNEH TORAH:
Hilchot Melachim –
Laws Concerning Kings

Chapter XI

1. The Messianic King will arise in the future and restore the Davidic Kingdom to its former state and original sovereignty. He will build the Sanctuary[1] and gather the dispersed of Israel.[2] All the laws will be re-instituted in his days as they had been aforetimes;[3] sacrifices will be offered, and the Sabbatical years and Jubilee years will be observed[4] fully as ordained by the Torah.[5]

---

1. See above, ch. II-A.
2. See above, ch. II-B. Note that the sequence stated is intentional: first the rebuilding of the *Bet Hamikdash* and then the complete ingathering of the exiles. This follows Psalms 147:2f., as interpreted in *Berachot* 49a; *Tanchuma,* Noach:11; and *Zohar* I:134a and 139a.
3. Isaiah 1:26. See *Sanhedrin* 51b, and Rashi there, *s.v.* verav Nachman, and Rambam's *Perush Hamishnah* on *Sanhedrin* 1:3.
4. *Mechilta deRashby* on Exodus 20:22; *Sifra* on Leviticus 2:14 *(parshata* 13:1).
5. Leviticus ch. 25. – Reinstituting the offering of sacrifices obviously requires the coming of Mashiach,

Anyone who does not believe in [Mashiach], or whoever does not look forward to his coming,[6] denies not only [the teachings of] the other prophets but [also those] of the Torah and of Moses our Teacher. For the Torah attested to him, as it is said:

> *"G-d, your G-d, will return your captivity and have mercy on you. He will return and gather you [from all the nations whither G-d, your G-d, has scattered you]. If your banished shall be at the utmost end of the heavens [G-d, your G-d, will gather you from there].. and G-d, your G-d, will bring you [to the land that your fathers possessed, and you will possess it].."*[7]

These words, explicitly stated in the Torah, include all the [Messianic] statements made by all the prophets.

---

as the rebuilding of the *Bet Hamikdash* is a prerequisite for the sacrifices. Likewise, Rambam makes specific reference to the observance of the *mitzvot* of the Sabbatical and Jubilee years as this, too, requires the coming of Mashiach: the ingathering of all the dispersed of Israel and their resettlement on their Divinely ordained territories is a prerequisite to observe these *mitzvot* "as ordained by the Torah;" see below, note 45.

6. See above, ch. V-A.
7. Deuteronomy 30:3-5. This prophecy has never yet been fulfilled, thus must relate to the Messianic redemption; see commentary of Ramban on Leviticus 26:16; and Abarbanel, *Mashmi'a Yeshu'ah* II:3.

There is reference [to this principle] also in the section of Bilam.[8] There he prophesied about the two *meshichim* (anointed ones): the first anointed one who is [King] David who saved Israel from the hand of their oppressors; and the final anointed one [i.e., Mashiach] who will arise from [the former's] descendants and save Israel in the end.[9] Thus it says there:

"I see him, but not now"[10] – this refers to David;

"I behold him, but not nigh"[10] – this refers to the Messianic King.

"A star steps out from Jacob"[10] – this refers to David;

"and a scepter will arise from Israel"[10] – this refers to the Messianic King.

"He will smite the great ones of Moab"[10] – this refers to David, as it says, "He smote Moab and measured them with a rope;"[11]

"and break all the children of Seth"[10] – this refers to the Messianic King, of whom it is said, "His rule will be from sea to sea."[12]

---

8. Numbers ch. 23-24. See the various Midrashim interpreting Bilam's prophecies; Rambam's *Igeret Teyman*, ch. 3; and *Mashmi'a Yeshu'ah*, s.v. Mevasser Harishon.
9. See *Midrash Aggadah*, Rashi, and R. Bachaya, on Numbers 24:17-18.
10. Numbers 24:17
11. II Samuels 8:2
12. Zechariah 9:10. The nations of the world are traced to Seth, the third son of Adam and Eve; "children of Seth" thus refers to these nations.

"Edom will be a possession"[13] – this refers to David, as it is said, "Edom became servants to David;[14]

"[and Seir] shall be a possession"[13] – this refers to the Messianic King, as it is said, "Saviors shall ascend Mount Zion [to judge the mount of Esau].."[15]

2. In context of the "cities of refuge," too, it says, *"When G-d, your G-d, will expand your borders.. you shall add three additional cities.."*[16] This has never yet taken place, and the Holy One, blessed is He, does not command anything in vain.[17]

---

13. Numbers 24:18
14. II Samuels 8:14
15. Obadiah 1:21
16. Deuteronomy 19:8-9. This passage refers to the future era when "your borders will be expanded" to include the lands of the Kenites, Kenizites, and Kadmonites (Genesis 15:19); see Rashi on this passage, based on *Sifre*, Re'ey, par. 75, and *Yerushalmi, Makot* 2:6. See Rambam, *Hilchot Rotze'ach* 8:4, for a detailed explanation. [See R. Chaim Vital, *Likutei Torah*, and *Sha'ar Hamitzvot*, on Deuteronomy 19:8-9; R. Isaiah Horowitz, *Shnei Luchot Haberit*, Bet David, p. 24a (ed. Warsaw, p. 17df.); R. Mosheh Alsheich, R. Shalom Shachna *(Siftei Kohen)*, and other commentators on Deut. 19:8-9; *Minchat Chinuch*, sect. 520; and *Likkutei Sichot*, vol. XXIV, p. 107ff.; on the need or significance of "cities of refuge" in the Messianic era.]
17. The lands of the Kenites, Kenizites and Kadmonites cannot be possessed by Israel until the Messianic era; *Yerushalmi, Kidushin* 1:end of 8; and *Bereishit Rabba* 44:23.

As for the [other] prophets' utterances [about Mashiach], there is no need for prooftexts as all the [prophets'] books are full of this concept.

3. Do not think that the Messianic King will have to perform signs and wonders and bring about novel things in the world, or resurrect the dead, and other such things. It is not so.[18] This is seen from the fact that Rabbi Akiva was a great sage, of the sages of the Mishnah, and he was an armor-bearer of King Bar Koziba[19] and said of him that he is the Messianic King: [R. Akiva] and all the wise men of his generation considered him to be the Messianic King until [Bar Koziba] was killed because of sins, and when he was killed they realized that he was not;[20] but the sages had not asked him for any sign or wonder.

The essence of all this is that this Torah [of ours], its statutes and its laws, are forever and all eternity, and nothing is to be added to them or diminished from them.[21]

---

18. Generally speaking, anyone claiming to be a prophet of G-d is tested by the fulfillment of his predictions (see Rambam, *Hilchot Yessodei Hatorah* ch. 10). The authenticity of Mashiach, however, is tested solely by the actual success of his Messianic activities, as explained in the sequel here and in paragraph 4 following.
19. Bar Kochba, who led a revolt against the Roman Empire to free the Holy Land.
20. See *Yerushalmi, Ta'anit* 4:5; *Eichah Rabba* 2:4 (and see there, in ed. Buber, note 57*).
21. Deuteronomy 4:2 and 13:1. Mashiach will thus not add anything to the Torah nor diminish from it; see Rambam's *Perush Hamishnah* cited above, note 3 (and *cf.* the sources cited above, p. 40 note 64).

(Whoever adds or diminishes anything, or interprets the Torah to change the plain sense of the commandments, is surely an impostor, wicked, and a heretic.)[22]

4. If a king arises from the House of David[23] who meditates on the Torah and occupies himself with the commandments like his ancestor David, in accordance with the written and oral Torah,[24] and he will prevail upon all of Israel to walk in [the ways of the Torah] and strengthen its

---

22. This bracketed paragraph appears only in the early editions of Rambam's code and was then omitted by Christian censors. The import is obvious: the ultimate test of a true messenger of G-d is total compliance with all the teachings of the Torah of Moses (see Deuteronomy 13:2*ff.* and *ibid.* 18:18*ff.*). The fact of anyone trying to tamper with the Torah of Moses – by adding, subtracting or changing anything – is the very proof that he is an impostor, regardless of any signs or wonders he may perform to verify his claims *(Hilchot Yessodei Hatorah* 8:3 and ch. 9-10; and see also *Igeret Teyman*, ch. 2). This passage, therefore, gives the lie to false prophets and pseudo-Messiahs of all times. There is only one criterion and test for the true Mashiach: total success in the fulfillment of all the Messianic prophecies within the context of the Torah. The next paragraph (especially in the full, uncensored version) elaborates further on the true nature and activities of the authentic Mashiach.
23. See above, ch. IV-A, notes 46-47.
24. *Midrash Tehilim* 2:9 and 110:4. *Cf.* above, ch. IV-A, note 48, and *ibid.*, sect. C.

breaches,[25] and he will fight the battles of G-d[26] — it may be assumed that he is Mashiach.[27]

If he did [these things] *successfully* (and defeated all the nations around him[27*]), built the Sanctuary on its site[28] and gathered the dispersed of Israel — he is definitely Mashiach![29] He will [then] correct the entire world to serve G-d in unity, as it is said, "For then I will turn to the peoples a pure tongue that all shall call upon the Name of G-d and serve Him with one consent."[30]

(If he did not succeed to that extent or was killed, it is clear that he is not the [Mashiach] promised by the Torah ... for all the prophets said that Mashiach is the redeemer of Israel and

---

25. That is, he will repair any breaches in the observance of the Torah.
26. The term "battles of G-d" has not only a literal meaning but also a figurative one, as in the sources cited in *Torah Shelemah* on Numbers 21:14, par. 84.
27. That is, he possesses the qualifications of Mashiach. *Cf.* above, ch. IV-B.
27*. I.e., defeating the oppressors and enemies of Israel. The bracketed phrase appears in the original editions but was omitted by gentile censors.
28. After the (first) *Bet Hamikdash* was built on its predetermined site on Mount Moriah (Temple Mount) in Jerusalem, that site is the exclusive location for the Sanctuary and the offering of sacrifices; *Megilah* 10a; *Zevachim* 112b. See Rambam, *Hilchot Bet Habechirah* 1:3 and 2:1-4.
29. As stated above (note 22), the actual success in all this is the only proof for the identity of Mashiach.
30. Zephaniah 3:9. See *Bereishit Rabba* 88:7; and above, ch. II-E.

their savior, and he gathers their dispersed and reinforces their commandments...)[31]

Chapter XII

1. One is not to presume that anything of the ways of the world will be set aside in the Messianic era, or that there will be any innovation in the order of creation; rather, the world will continue according to its norms.[32]

---

31. The bracketed passage is an excerpt from a lengthy sequel which appears only in the early editions of the code and was then omitted by Christian censors. The thrust is again on the distinction between the true Messiah and the various impostors who come with Messianic claims (see above, note 22). The entire passage elaborates specifically on Judaism's rejection of the claims made by the founders of Christianity and Islam. At the same time it explains also that by the mysterious ways of Providence, the followers of these two have helped pave the way for the Messianic age by acquainting the world with the principle of Mashiach, the Torah and the commandments; "these doctrines have been spread to distant isles and many nations of uncircumcised hearts, and they discuss these matters and the precepts of the Torah." At present, though, these nations' perception of these concepts, based on the false interpretations of those religions, is erroneous; but when the true Mashiach will come "all of them will recant and realize that their ancestors endowed them with falsehood, and that their prophets and ancestors misled them." [Note that this premise of the Providential design of history was stated already by R. Yehudah Halevi in *Kuzary* IV:23.]
32. See below, paragraph 2, note 37.

As for that which is said in Isaiah, that "the wolf will dwell with the sheep and the leopard will lie down with the kid"[33] – this is an allegory and metaphor. It means that Israel shall dwell securely alongside the wicked heathens who are likened to wolves and leopards, as it is said "a wolf from the plains ravages, a leopard lies in wait over their cities."[34] [In the Messianic era] all will return to the true religion and will neither steal nor destroy, but consume that which is permitted, in repose alongside Israel, as it is said, "the lion will eat straw like the ox."[35] All other such expressions are also allegories, and in the era of the Messianic King everyone will come to know what the allegory is about and what allusions are indicated.[36]

2. The sages said: "There is no difference between the present age and the Messianic era but [delivery from] subjection to foreign powers."[37]

From the plain sense of the words of the prophets it is apparent that in the beginning of the Messianic era will occur the war of Gog and Magog;[38] and that prior to the war of Gog and Magog a prophet will arise to correct Israel and

---

33. Isaiah 11:6. *Cf.* above, ch. II-F.
34. Jeremiah 5:6. *Cf. Bereishit Rabba* 99:2.
35. Isaiah 11:7 and 65:25.
36. In his *Ma'amar Techiyat Hametim*, sect. 6, Rambam qualifies this allegorical interpretation as a personal opinion. Though convinced of his view, he allows for the possibility that these prophecies may in fact be literal as understood by most other authorities. See above, ch. II-H, note 23.
37. *Berachot* 34b. See above, ch. II-H, note 23.
38. *Avodah Zara* 3b. See Appendix I, note 2.

to prepare their hearts, as it is said, "Behold, I am sending you the prophet Elijah [before the coming of the great and awesome day of G-d]."[39] He will not come to declare the pure impure or the impure pure, nor to disqualify people presumed to be of legitimate lineage or to legitimize those presumed to be of disqualified lineage;[40] but to establish peace in the world, as it is said, "He will turn the heart of the fathers to the children.."[41]

Some sages say that Elijah will come *before* the coming of Mashiach.[42]

All these and similar matters, however, man will not know how they will occur until they come to pass; for in the [statements of the] prophets these are undefined matters, and the sages, too, do not have a clear tradition on these subjects except for the [apparent] implications of the Scriptural verses. That is why they have differences of opinion in these matters. In any case, neither the sequence of these events nor their details are fundamental to the faith.

A person should not involve himself with the homiletical statements – or protract on the Midrashim – speaking of these or similar matters,

---

39. Malachi 3:23. *Yerushalmi, Shabbat* 1:3, and *ibid. Shekalim* 3:3; see Appendix I, note 6.
40. That is, he will not change legal decisions of the past which may have been based on error. "Lineage" (*yichus*) refers to the determination of pedigree in context of the prohibition of intermarriage with people of "tainted lineage" (e.g., Deuteronomy 23:3-9; and see *Kidushin* 69a).
41. Malachi 3:24. See *Eduyot* 8:7.
42. *Eruvin* 43b; *Pesikta Rabaty* 36:4. See Appendix I.

nor is one to consider them fundamental; for they do not lead to either fear or love [of G-d].[43]

Likewise, one is not to calculate "ends" [dates of the Messianic redemption]. The sages said, "May the spirit expire of those who calculate the 'ends.'"[44] Rather, one is to await [the redemption] and believe the principle of this matter as we have explained.

3. In the era of the Messianic King, when his kingdom will be established and all of Israel will gather around him, all of them will have their pedigree determined by him,[45] by means of the

---

43. The belief in — and the awaiting of — Mashiach is fundamental to the Jewish faith. Determination of the specific details of events that occur with the coming of Mashiach, or the precise sequence of such, have no practical bearing upon our faith or behavior. There is then no point in trying to resolve these issues. As Rambam puts it elsewheres, there is no point in issuing decisive rulings or resolutions in controversies that are essentially speculative and do not affect actual behavior; see his commentary on *Sotah* 3:3 and *Shevu'ot* 1:4; and cf. *Tossafot Yom Tov* on *Berachot* 5:4.

44. *Sanhedrin* 97b. See above, ch. V, note 75.

45. Tribal pedigree or affiliation. The determination of tribal pedigree and affiliation is important for the proper resettlement of all the tribes in their Divinely assigned territories in the Holy Land (see Numbers 26:52-55 and 33:54-34:1ff.; Joshua ch. 18-21) which has Halachic implications as a prerequisite for the observance of the Sabbatical and Jubilee-years (see above, note 5); see *Arachin* 32b, and Rambam, *Hilchot Shemitah Veyovel* 10:8-9. (Cf. also *Hilchot Terumah* 1:26, and *Hilchot Bikurim* 5:5, for other *mitzvot* dependent on this condition.) Tribal

Holy Spirit that will rest upon him, as it is said, "He will sit as a refiner and purifier."[46] First he will purify the descendants of Levi,[47] saying "This one is a legitimate *Kohen* (priest), and this one is a legitimate Levite," while diverting those of improper lineage to the [rank of] Israelites.[48] Thus it is said, "The governor [Nechemiah] said to them .. until there will rise a *Kohen* with the Urim and Tumim;"[49] from this you can infer that the determination of presumed pedigree and the public declaration of lineage is by means of the Holy Spirit.[50]

---

    affiliation also has implications for the practice of individual rites, such as liturgy; see *Zohar* III: 170a (discussed at length in my *The Great Maggid*, ch. X, pp. 151-9, see the sources cited there).

    Moreover, legitimate membership in the tribe of Levi specifically is of utmost importance as the Torah ordains special functions for *Kohanim* (priests) and *Leviyim* (Levites) respectively, to be carried out by them exclusively; see Rambam, *Hilchot Klei Hamikdash Veha'ovdim Bo*, ch. 3-4.

46. Malachi 3:3
47. *Kidushin* 70bf. The tribe of Levi divides into the two groups of *Kohanim* and *Leviyim*, each of which is sanctified and charged with its own exclusive tasks; see note 45.
48. All Jews who do not qualify as legitimate *Kohanim* or *Leviyim* are automatically classified as *Yisra'elim* (regular Israelites).
49. Ezra 2:63.
50. The verse cited refers to the examination of those who ascended from the Babylonian exile with Ezra and Nechemiah in order to determine legitimate *Kohanim* for the service in the second *Bet Hamikdash*. Those unable to produce genealogical registers of their

As for the Israelites, he will only determine their tribal lineage, that is, he will inform that "this one is of such-and-such a tribe and that one is of such-and-such a tribe."[51] He will not pronounce on those presumed to be of legitimate ancestry that "this one is a *mamzer* and that one is a 'slave';"[52] for the law stipulates

---

priesthood were told that they could not be accepted as *Kohanim* until their status could be determined with certainty by a *"kohen* with the Urim and Tumim." (Ezra 2:61-63; see *Kidushin* 69b, and the commentaries there.) The Urim and Tumim were part of the High Priest's garbs, invested with oracular power of the Holy Spirit (see Rashi on Exodus 28:30; *Yoma* 73b). This power was no longer extant after the first *Bet Hamikdash* and will be restored only with the coming of Mashiach *(Sotah* 48a-b*)*. Ezra and Nechemiah, therefore, could not resolve cases of doubtful priesthood, for this requires prophetic power. Mashiach, however, will be able to do so by means of the Holy Spirit that will rest upon him *(cf.* above, ch. IV-C*)*.

51. As stated in note 45, this has important implications of practical relevance.

52. *Eduyot* 8:7. It is quite possible that people of illegitimate ancestry (e.g., *mamzerim* i.e., offspring of incestuous and certain adulterous unions; or offspring of "slaves" i.e., of non-Jewish slaves who had not converted fully to Judaism), intermarriage with which is forbidden to Jews (see note 40), may have become absorbed in the Jewish community in the course of time without anyone aware of their true status. Mashiach will not pronounce judgment on them for the reason following.

that once a family is intermixed [with the Jewish community at large] it remains intermixed.[53]

4. The sages and the prophets did not long for the Messianic era so that they may rule over the whole world or dominate the heathens, nor to be exalted by the nations, nor in order that they may eat, drink and be merry; but only to be free [for involvement] with the Torah and its wisdom, without anyone to oppress and disturb them, so that they may merit the life of the World-to-Come, as we explained in *Hilchot Teshuvah*.[54]

5. In that era there will be neither famine[55] nor war,[56] neither envy nor strife,[57] because good will emanate in abundance and all delightful things will be accessible as dust.[58] The one preoccupation of the entire world will be solely to know G-d. The Israelites, therefore, will be great sages and know the hidden matters,[59] and they will attain knowledge of their Creator to the extent of human capacity, as it is said: *"The earth*

---

53. *Kidushin* 71a. All such people will thus enjoy the benefit of doubt and remain legitimate members of the community.
54. *Hilchot Teshuvah* 9:2. See above, end of ch. II-H (and notes 24-28 there), and ch. IV, notes 63-66.
55. See above, ch. II-H, and notes 19-21 there.
56. See above, ch. II-F.
57. *Berachot* 17a
58. See above, ch. II-H, notes 19-21; and *cf. Midrash Tehilim* 87:3. "Accessible like dust" implies not only over-abundant plentitude, but also a refined sense of priorities in which worldly delights will be regarded like dust.
59. Things presently hidden and unknown; see above, ch. IV-C, notes 63-64.

shall be full with the knowledge of G-d as the waters cover the sea!"[60]

---

60. Isaiah 11:9; see above, ch. II-D.

Appendix I
The Prophet Elijah: Harbinger of the Redemption

The Messianic redemption is closely associated with the name of the prophet Elijah. He is regarded as the forerunner of Mashiach, "the harbinger who will proclaim peace, the harbinger of good who will proclaim salvation, saying to Zion 'Your G-d reigns!'" (Isaiah 52:7)[1]

Rambam writes: "Before the war of Gog and Magog[2] a prophet will arise to rectify Israel and

---

1. See *Pesikta Rabaty* 36:4 (ed. Friedmann, ch. 35).
2. A climactic battle (see Ezekiel ch. 38-39) in the early stages of the Messianic redemption (see *Igeret Teyman*, end of ch. 3) against the forces of evil. (In *Tanchuma*, Korach: end of 14, there seems to be an allusion that it may involve all the nations of the world.) These forces presumptuously undertake to battle not only Israel but the Almighty Himself, as it were, and will suffer an appropriate defeat. Even so, for a while it will be a most traumatic event with great trials and tribulations for Israel. See *Agadat Bereishit* 2:1; *Midrash Tehilim* 2:4; and the parallel passages cited there. See also *Targum Yehonathan* (and

prepare their hearts, as it is said, 'Behold, I am sending you the prophet Elijah [before the coming of the *great and awesome day of G-d*]' (Malachi 3:23).. Some of the sages say that Elijah will come before the coming of Mashiach."[3]

The apparent conflict of opinions is most readily resolved in terms of the tradition that Elijah will make *two* appearances: first he will appear with the coming of Mashiach; then he will be concealed to appear again before the war of Gog and Magog.[4] The phrase "great and awesome day of G-d" is thus read (a) as a reference to the day of Mashiach's coming, stating that Elijah will come prior to this to announce and proclaim his coming;[5] and (b) as a reference to the awesome day of the war of Gog and Magog and Elijah's involvement with the resurrection of the dead.[6]

The prophet Elijah's functions will thus include: to rectify Israel's behavior, causing them to return to G-d with *teshuvah,* as a preparation for the Messianic redemption;[7] to proclaim the

---

Targum Yerushalmi) on Numbers 11:26; and *Torah Shelemah* on this verse, note 196. See, though, below, Appendix II, note 17.

3. *Hilchot Melachim* 12:2
4. *Seder Olam Rabba,* ch. 17. *Yalkut Shimoni,* Melachim:par. 207. *Cf.* Radal on *Pirkei deR. Eliezer,* ch. 43, note 85. For another approach and resolution, see *Chidushim Ubi'urim Behilchot Melachim,* sect. IV.
5. *Eruvin* 43b; *Pesikta Rabaty* 36:4.
6. *Berayta deR. Pinchas ben Yair,* appended at end of *Sotah; Yerushalmi, Shabbat* 1:3. See Ran on *Avodah Zara* 20b, *s.v.* Biyerushalmi.
7. *Pirkei deR. Eliezer,* end of ch. 43. *Cf.* Rambam's commentary on *Eduyot* 8:7.

imminent coming of Mashiach;[8] to restore the sacred objects placed in the Holy of Holies of the first *Bet Hamikdash,* and later hidden by King Josiah[9] before its destruction;[10] and to be involved with the resurrection of the dead.[11] Above all, the essential task of Elijah will be to resolve legal disputes and to establish peace in the world, as it is said, "He will turn the heart of the fathers to the children, and the heart of the children to their fathers." (Malachi 3:24)[12]

---

8. Note, though, that even according to the sources cited above note 5, this need not be, and Mashiach may come even without any prior announcement by Elijah; see *Otzar Balum* on *Ayn Ya'akov, Sanhedrin* 98a; Responsa *Chatam Sofer,* vol. VI:no. 98; and *Keren Orah* on *Nazir* 66a. *Cf. Chidushim Ubi'urim Behilchot Melachim,* III:17, and IV:9; and the sources cited there.
9. *Yoma* 52b; *Horayot* 12a.
10. *Mechilta,* Beshalach, Vayasa:ch. 5.
11. See above, note 6.
12. *Eduyot* 8:7; *Hilchot Melachim* 12:2. *Cf. Encyclopedia Talmudit, s.v.* Eliyahu.

Appendix II
Mashiach Ben Yossef

Jewish tradition speaks of two redeemers, each one called Mashiach. Both are involved in ushering in the Messianic era. They are *Mashiach ben David* and *Mashiach ben Yossef*.[1]

The term *Mashiach* unqualified always refers to *Mashiach ben David* (Mashiach the descendant of David) of the tribe of Judah. He is the actual (final) redeemer who shall rule in the Messianic age. All that was said in our text relates to him.

Mashiach ben Yossef (Mashiach the descendant of Joseph) of the tribe of Ephraim (son of Joseph), is also referred to as *Mashiach ben Ephrayim*, Mashiach the descendant of Ephraim.[2] He will come first, before the final

---

1. See *Sukah* 52b; *Zohar* I:25b; *ibid.* II:120a, III:153b, 246b and 252a. (See *Sha'arei Zohar* on *Sukah* 52a for further relevant sources in the *Zohar*-writings.)
2. *Sukah* 52a-b; *Zohar* I:25b; *ibid.* III:246b and 252b etc.; and *Midrash Agadat Mashiach*; use the term *Mashiach ben Yossef*. *Targum Yehonathan* on Exodus

redeemer, and later will serve as his viceroy.³

The essential task of Mashiach ben Yossef is to act as precursor to Mashiach ben David: he will prepare the world for the coming of the final

---

40:11; *Zohar* II:120a; *ibid.* 153b, 194b, and 243b etc.; *Midrash Tehilim* 60:3; and other Midrashim refer to *Mashiach ben Ephrayim*. *Pesikta Rabaty*, ch. 36-37 (ed. Friedmann, ch. 35-36) refers to *Ephrayim Meshiach Tzidki* (Ephraim, My righteous Mashiach); the term Ephraim, though, may relate here to collective Israel, thus referring to Mashiach ben David.

Pirkei Heichalot Rabaty, ch. 39 *(Batei Midrashot*, ed. Wertheimer, vol. I)* and *Sefer Zerubavel (ibid.*, vol. II)*, offer his personal name as Nechemiah ben Chushiel (likewise in *Midrash Tehilim* 60:3), adding "who is of Ephraim the son of Joseph." (Interestingly enough, *Pirkei deR. Eliezer*, ch. 19, calls him Menachem ben Ammi'el, the very name the other sources – and *Zohar* III:173b – attribute to Mashiach ben David.)

Targum Yehonathan on Exodus 40:11 traces his descent to Joshua (*cf.* below, note 7). Other sources state that he is a descendant of Yeravam ben Nevat, with practical implications in the Providential scheme for this genealogy; see *Zohar Chadash*, Balak:56b; commentary of R. Abraham Galante on *Zohar* II:120a (cited in *Or Hachamah* there); and *Emek Hamelech*, Sha'ar Olam Hatohu:ch. 46. *Cf Devash Lefi*, *s.v.* mem:par. 18. (Note also the sources cited in *Sha'arei Zohar* on *Sukah* 52a with regards to other views about his lineage.)

3. The harmony and cooperation between Mashiach ben David and Mashiach ben Yossef signifies the total unity of Israel, removing the historical rivalries between the tribes of Judah and Joseph; see Isaiah 11:13 and Rashi

redeemer. Different sources attribute to him different functions, some even charging him with tasks traditionally associated with Mashiach ben David (such as the ingathering of the exiles, the rebuilding of the *Bet Hamikdash*, and so forth).[4]

The principal and final function ascribed to Mashiach ben Yossef is of political and military nature. He shall wage war against the forces of evil that oppress Israel. More specifically, he will do battle against Edom, the descendants of Esau.[5] Edom is the comprehensive designation of the enemies of Israel,[6] and it will be crushed through

---

there. (*Cf. Bereishit Rabba* 70:15; and *Torah Shelemah* on Genesis 29:16, note 49.)

4. See *Pirkei Heichalot Rabaty*, ch. 39; *Sefer Zerubavel*; *Midrash Agadat Mashiach* (most of which is quoted in *Lekach Tov*, Balak, on Numbers 24:17*ff*.); and *cf.* Rashi on *Sukah* 52b, *s.v.* charashim. See also Ramban, Commentary on Song 8:13.

5. Note that the final battle of Mashiach ben Yossef is said to be against Armilus, ruler of Edom. See the Messianic Midrashim *Zerubavel; Agadat Mashiach; Vayosha* etc. (Specific references are offered in R. Margolius, *Malachei Elyon*, part II, *s.v.* Armilas; and see also the sources cited below, notes 18-19.)

6. Edom is the perpetual enemy of Israel (see *Sifre*, Beha'alotecha, par. 69, cited by Rashi on Genesis 33:4; and see also *Megilah* 6a) and its final foe: the present *galut* is referred to as the *galut* of Edom (see *Bereishit Rabba* 44:17; *Vayikra Rabba* 13:5; and parallel passages) and Edom will be defeated ultimately by Mashiach (Obadiah; *Yoma* 10a; *Midrash Tehilim* 6:2; and *cf. Tanchuma*, Bo:4).

Interestingly enough, according to *Pirkei deR. Eliezer* ch. 28 (in non-censored versions), the Ishmaelites (Arabs) will be the final kingdom to be

the progeny of Joseph. Thus it was prophesied of old, "The House of Jacob will be a fire and the House of Joseph a flame, and the House of Esau for stubble.." (Obadiah 1:18): "the progeny of Esau shall be delivered only into the hands of the progeny of Joseph."[7]

This ultimate confrontation between Joseph and Esau is alluded already in the very birth of Joseph when his mother Rachel exclaimed, "G-d has taken away my disgrace" (Genesis 30:23): with prophetic vision she foresaw that an "anointed savior" will descend from Joseph and

---

defeated by Mashiach. Other sources state "Edom and Ishmael" (see *Torah Shelemah* on Genesis 15:12, note 130). Note, however, *Pirkei deR. Eliezer*, ch. 44 (and *cf. Midrash Tehilim* 2:6 and 83:3) that Edom and Ishmael have become intermingled. See also *Mayanei Hayeshu'ah*, Mayan 11:8.

7. *Baba Batra* 123b. *Targum Yehonathan* on Genesis 30:23. *Tanchuma*, ed. Buber, Vayetze:15; and *Bereishit Rabba* 73:7; and the parallel passages cited there. See *Bereishit Rabba* 99:2, that Edom shall fall by the *meshu'ach milchamah* (the one anointed for battle; see below, note 10 for this term) who will be descended from Joseph.

Mashiach ben Yossef's battle against Edom is analogous to, and the culmination of, Israel's first battle against Edom (Amalek) after the exodus from Egypt (Exodus 17:5*ff.*). In that first battle, the Jewish army was led by Joshua – who is also of the tribe of Ephraim, and (according to some) this Mashiach's ancestor (see above note 2); see Ramban on Exodus 17:9, and R. Bachaya on Exodus 18:1. *Cf.* also R. Bachaya on Exodus 1:5, drawing an analogy between the role of Joseph in Egypt and the role of the

that he will remove the disgrace of Israel.[8] In this context she called his name *'Yossef,* saying *'yossef Hashem* – may G-d add to me *ben acher* (lit., another son), i.e., *ben acharono shel olam* – one who will be at the end of the world's time,'[9] from which it follows that *'meshu'ach milchamah* – one anointed for battle' will descend from Joseph."[10]

The immediate results of this war[11] will be disastrous: Mashiach ben Yossef will be killed.

Mashiach descended from him in the ultimate redemption.

8. The Messianic aspect is derived by analogy with Isaiah 4:1.
9. The Messianic aspect is derived by analogy with Genesis 4:25 which in *Agadat Mashiach* (cited in *Lekach Tov* on Numbers 24:17) is put into Messianic context.
10. *Midrash Yelamdenu,* cited in *Kuntres Acharon* of *Yalkut Shimoni.* (This *Kuntres Acharon* appears only in very few editions of *Yalkut Shimoni,* but was republished in Jellinek's *Bet Hamidrash,* vol. VI. Our passage appears there on p. 81, par. 20; and is also cited in *Torah Shelemah* on Genesis 30:23-24, par. 84 and 89.)

    In context of his military function, Mashiach ben Yossef is referred to as *meshu'ach milchamah (cf. Sotah* 42a, and Rashi on Deuteronomy 20:2, for this term); see *Bereishit Rabba* 75:6 and 99:2; *Shir Rabba* 2:13 (a parallel passage of *Sukah* 52b); and *Agadat Bereishit,* ch. (63) 64.
11. *Targum Yehonathan* on Exodus 40:11, and on Zechariah 12:10 (manuscript-version in ed. A. Sperber); *Agadat Mashiach*; *Pirkei Heichalot Rabaty* (in version cited by Ramban, *Sefer Hage'ulah,* sha'ar IV; ed. Chavel, p. 291); and Rashi on *Sukah* 52a;

This is described in the prophecy of Zechariah, who says of this tragedy that "they shall mourn him as one mourns for an only child." (Zechariah 12:10).[12] His death will be followed by a period of great calamities. These new tribulations shall be the final test for Israel, and shortly thereafter Mashiach ben David shall come, avenge his death, resurrect him, and inaugurate the Messianic era of everlasting peace and bliss.[13]

This, in brief, is the general perception of the "second Mashiach," the descendant of Joseph through the tribe of Ephraim.

Quite significantly, R. Saadiah Gaon (one of the few to elaborate on the role of Mashiach ben Yossef) notes that this sequence is not definite but *contingent!* Mashiach ben Yossef will *not* have to appear before Mashiach ben David, nor will the activities attributed to him or his death have to occur. All depends on the spiritual condition of the Jewish people at the time the redemption is to take place:

---

    identify the battle of Mashiach ben Yossef with the war of Gog and Magog.

12. *Sukah* 52a, and parallel passages.
13. *Pirkei Heichalot Rabaty*, ch. 39 (cited in *Sefer Hage'ulah*, sha'ar IV); *Sefer Zerubavel*; *Agadat Mashiach* (cited in *Lekach Tov, ibid.*). See R. Saadiah Gaon, *Emunot Vede'ot* VIII:ch. 5, adding Scriptural "prooftexts" or allusions for all details; and the lengthy responsum of R. Hai Gaon on the redemption, published in *Otzar Hageonim* on *Sukah* 52a, and in *Midreshei Ge'ulah*, ed. Y. Ibn Shemuel, p. 135*ff*. Cf. Rashi and Ibn Ezra on Zechariah 12:10; Ibn Ezra and Redak on Zechariah 13:7.

The essential function of Mashiach ben Yossef is to prepare Israel for the final redemption, to put them into the proper condition in order to clear the way for Mashiach ben David to come. Of that ultimate redemption it is said, that if Israel repent (return to G-d) they shall be redeemed immediately (even before the predetermined date for Mashiach's coming). If they will not repent and thus become dependent on the final date, "the Holy One, blessed be He, will set up a ruler over them, whose decrees shall be as cruel as Haman's, thus causing Israel to repent, and thereby bringing them back to the right path."[14] In other words, if Israel shall return to G-d on their own and make themselves worthy of the redemption, there is *no need* for the trials and tribulations associated with the above account of events related to Mashiach ben Yossef. Mashiach ben David will come directly and redeem us.[15]

Moreover, even if there be a need for the earlier appearance of Mashiach ben Yossef, the consequences need not be as severe as described. Our present prayers and meritorious actions can mitigate these. R. Isaac Luria *(Ari-zal)* notes that the descendant of Joseph, by being the precursor of the ultimate Mashiach, is in effect *kissey David*, the "seat" or "throne" of David, i.e., of Mashiach. Thus when praying in the daily *Amidah*, "speedily establish the throne of Your servant David," one should consider that this refers to Mashiach ben Yossef and beseech G-d

---

14. *Sanhedrin* 97b
15. *Emunot Vede'ot* VIII:6; see there at length. *Cf. Or Hachayim* on Numbers 24:17.

that he should not die in the Messianic struggle.[16] As all prayers, this one, too, will have its effect.

It follows, then, that all the above is not an essential or unavoidable part of the Messianic redemption that we await. Indeed, it – (and the same may be said of the climactic war of Gog and Magog) – may occur *(or may have occured already!)* in modified fashion.[17] This may explain why Rambam does not mention anything about Mashiach ben Yossef. R. Saadiah Gaon[18] and R.

---

16. *Peri Eitz Chayim*, Sha'ar Ha'amidah:ch. 19; and *Siddur Ha-Ari*; on this blessing. The Ari's teaching is cited in *Or Hachayim* on Leviticus 14:9, see there (and also on Numbers 24:17, where he relates this prayer to the next blessing of the *Amidah*); and see also *Even Shelemah*, ch. 11, note 6. *Cf. Zohar* II:120a (and *Or Hachamah* there), and *ibid.* III:153b. See next note.

17. The battle of Gog and Magog (see above, Appendix I, note 2) is another of the complex issues of the Messianic redemption. In fact, an authoritative tradition from the disciples of the Baal Shem Tov states that the extraordinary length of the present severe *galut* has already made up for the troubles of that battle and the trauma of the death of Mashiach ben Yossef, so that these will no longer occur; see R. Shemuel of Sochachev, *Shem MiShemuel*, Vayigash, *s.v.* Vayigash 5677 (*s.v.* venireh od, p. 298b*f.*).

18. *Emunot Vede'ot* VIII:ch. 5-6. See also the commentary on Shir Hashirim attributed to R. Saadiah Gaon, published in *Chamesh Megilot im Perushim Atikim (Miginzei Teyman)*, ed. Y. Kapach, on Song 7:12-14 (p. 115; and also in *Midreshei Ge'ulah*, p. 131*f.*; as noted already by the editors, this passage is most probably based on *Sefer Zerubavel*).

Hai Gaon,[19] as well as a good number of commentators, do refer to him briefly or at length. In view of the divergent Midrashim and interpretations on this subject it is practically impossible to present a more definitive synopsis that would go far beyond the above. Thus it is wisest to cite and follow R. Chasdai Crescas who states that "no certain knowledge can be derived from the interpretations of the prophecies about Mashiach ben Yossef, nor from the statements about him by some of the Geonim;" there is no point, therefore, in elaborating on the subject.[20]

---

19. See his extensive responsum, cited above note 13.
20. *Or Hashem*, Ma'amar III, klal 8: end of ch. 1.

BIBLIOGRAPHY

Bibliography Of Texts Cited*

Arba Me'ot Shekel Kessef, R. Chaim Vital, Tel Aviv 1964

Avnei Nezer, see *Teshuvot Avnei Nezer*

Bachaya al Hatorah, R. Bachaya ben Asher, Jerusalem 1959

Batei Midrashot, ed. R. Shlomo A. Wertheimer, Jerusalem 1952-3

Bartenura, see *Perush Bartenura*

Bet Elokim, R. Mosheh of Tirani (Mabit), Warsaw 1813

Besha'ah Shehikdimu – 5672, R. Sholom Dov-Ber of Lubavitch, Brooklyn NY 1977

Bet Ha-Midrash, ed. A. Jellinek, Jerusalem 1967

Bnei Yisas'char, R. Tzvi Elimelech of Dinov, Brooklyn NY 1984

Chafetz Chaim al Hasiddur, R. Israel Meir Hakohen, Jerusalem 1959

Chafetz Chaim al Hatorah, R. Israel Meir Hakohen, New York NY n.d.

---

* For texts beyond *Tnach* (the Biblical Books), Talmud, Midrashim, and their standard commentaries

Chamesh Megilot im Perushim Atikim [Miginzei Teyman], ed. J. Kapach, Jerusalem 1962

Chatam Sofer al Hatorah, R. Mosheh Sofer, ed. J. N. Stern, Jerusalem 1978. See also *Teshuvot Chatam Sofer*

Chessed LeAvraham, R. Abraham Azulay, Lemberg 1863

Chidushim Ubi'urim Behilchot Melachim, R. Menachem M. Schneerson of Lubavitch, Brooklyn NY 1991

Chizuk Emunah, see *Chafetz Chaim al Hatorah*

Darkei Chayim Veshalom (Munkatsh), ed. J. M. Gold, Jerusalem 1970

Devash Lefi, R. Chaim Joseph David Azulay, Jerusalem 1962

Eitz Chayim, R. Chaim Vital, ed. Warsaw, Tel Aviv 1975

Emek Hamelech, R. Naftali Hertz, ed. Amsterdam, Bnei Brak 1973

Emunot Vede'ot, R. Saadiah Gaon, Josefow 1885

Even Shelemah (Teachings of R. Elijah, the Vilna Gaon, ed. R. Shmuel Maltzan, Jerusalem 1960

Hagadah shel Pesach Mibet Levi [Brisk], ed. M. Gerlitz, Jerusalem 1983

Hilchot Bet Habechirah, see *Mishneh Torah*

Hilchot De'ot, see *Mishneh Torah*

Hilchot Klei Hamikdash, see *Mishneh Torah*

Hilchot Matnot Aniyim, see *Mishneh Torah*

Hilchot Melachim, see *Mishneh Torah*

Hilchot Rotze'ach, see *Mishneh Torah*

Hilchot Teshuvah, see *Mishneh Torah*

Hilchot Yessodei Hatorah, see *Mishneh Torah*

Igeret Teyman, see *Igrot Harambam*

Igrot Harambam, standard editions, and ed. Kapach, Jerusalem 1972

Ikkarim, R. Joseph Albo, Vilna n.d.

Keter Shem Tov (Teachings of R. Israel Baal Shem Tov), Brooklyn NY 1972

Kuntres Be'inyan "Torah Chadashah Me'iti Tetze", R. Menachem M. Schneerson of Lubavitch, Brooklyn NY 1991

Kuntres Perush Hamilot, R. Dov Ber of Lubavitch, Brooklyn NY 1975

Likkutei Sichot, R. Menachem M. Schneerson of Lubavitch, Brooklyn NY 1962*ff*.

Likutei Torah Veta'amei Hamitzvot, R. Chaim Vital, Tel Aviv 1963

Ma'amar Techiyat Hametim, see *Igrot Harambam*

Ma'amar Torah Or, R. Israel Meir Hakohen, in *Assifat Zekenim*, Warsaw 1902

Ma'amarei Admur Hazaken – Et'halech, R. Shneur Zalman of Liadi, Brooklyn, N.Y. 1957

Maamarei Admur Hazaken – Haketzarim, R. Shneur Zalman of Liadi, Brooklyn, N.Y. 1981

Maggid Devarav Leya'akov, R. Dov Ber of Mezhirech, Brooklyn NY 1972

Malachei Elyon, R. Reuven Margolius, Jerusalem 1964

Margaliyot Hayam, R. Reuven Margolius, Jerusalem 1958

Mashmi'a Yeshu'ah, R. Yitzchak Abarbanel, Tel Aviv 1960

Mayanei Hayeshu'ah, R. Yitzchak Abarbanel, Tel Aviv 1960

Mayim Rabim – 5636, R. Shmuel of Lubavitch, Brooklyn NY 1946

Midbar Kedemot, R. Chaim Joseph David Azulay, Jerusalem 1962

Midreshei Ge'ulah, ed. Y. Ibn Shemuel, Jerusalem 1954

Minchat Chinuch, R. Joseph Babad, New York NY 1962

Mishneh Torah, R. Mosheh ben Maimon (Rambam), standard ed.

Netzach Yisrael, R. Judah Loewe (Maharal), New York NY 1961

Or Hachamah, ed. R. Abraham Azulay, Przemysl 1896

Or Hashem, R. Chasdai Crescas, Tel Aviv 1963

Or Hatorah – Na"ch, R. Menachem Mendel *(Tzemach Tzedek)* of Lubavitch, Brooklyn NY 1969

Peri Eitz Chayim, R. Chaim Vital, Jerusalem 1960

Peri Tzadik, R. Tzadok Hakohen, Jerusalem 1972

Perush Bartenura – Megilat Ruth, R. Ovadiah of Bartenura, appended to *Mikra'ot Gedolot – Bamidbar*

Perush Hamishnah, R. Mosheh ben Maimon, ed. Kapach, Jerusalem 1963-9

Petach Einayim, R. Chaim Joseph David Azulay, Jerusalem n.d.

Principles of the Faith, see *Perush Hamishnah*

Roke'ach, R. Eleazar of Worms, Warsaw 1880

Sdei Chemed, R. Chaim Chizkiahu Medini, Brooklyn NY 1959

Sefer Hage'ulah, R. Mosheh ben Nachman (Ramban), in *Kitvei Ramban*, ed. C. Chavel, Jerusalem 1963

Sefer Hamitzvot, R. Moshen ben Maimon, Jerusalem 1959

Semak (Amudei Golah: Sefer Mitzvot Katan), R. Yitzchak of Corbeil, New York NY 1959

Sha'ar Ha'emunah, R. Dov Ber of Lubavitch, Brooklyn NY 1974

Sha'ar Hagemul, R. Mosheh ben Nachman, in *Kitvei Ramban*, ed. C. Chavel, Jerusalem 1963

Sha'ar Hagilgulim, R. Chaim Vital, Tel Aviv 1963

Sha'ar Hamitzvot, R. Chaim Vital, Tel Aviv 1962

Sha'ar Hapesukim, R. Chaim Vital, Tel Aviv 1962

Sha'arei Zohar, R. Reuven Margolius, Jerusalem 1956

Shem MiShemuel, R. Shmuel of Sochachev, Jerusalem 1974

Shibalei Haleket, R. Tzidkiyah dei Mansi, New York NY 1959

Shnei Luchot Haberit, R. Isaiah Horowitz, Jerusalem 1963

Siddur Ha-Ari [Seder Tefilah mikol Hashanah], R. Shabtai of Rashkov, (Koretz 1797)

Tanya, R. Shneur Zalman of Liadi, Brooklyn NY 1954

Teshuvot Avnei Nezer, R. Abraham of Sochachev, New York NY n.d.

Teshuvot Chatam Sofer, R. Mosheh Sofer, Brooklyn NY 1958

Teshuvot Min Hashamayim, R. Jacob of Marvege, ed. R. Margolius, Jerusalem 1957

Teshuvot Radvaz, R. David ibn Zimra, New York NY 1967

Teshuvot Ubi'urim, R. Menachem M. Schneerson of Lubavitch, Brooklyn NY 1974

Torah Shelemah, ed. R. Menachem M. Kasher, New York NY 1957*ff*.

Tossafot Harosh al Hatorah, R. Asher ben Yechiel, Jerusalem 1963

Tzipita Liyeshu'ah, R. Israel Meir Hakohen, Tel Aviv 1929

Yeshu'ot Meshicho, R. Yitzchak Abarbanel, Koenigsburg 1861

לזכר וע"נ
מו"ח איש חי רב פעלים
עוסק בצ"צ באמונה
מתלמידיו של אהרן
החבר מו"ה
אברהם
בן
מוהר"ר נתן ומרת רעכלא
זלה"ה
עלזאס
שבק חיים לכל חי יו"ד ניסן ה'תנש"א

לזכות
כ״ק אדמו״ר שליט״א

May the Torah and the prayers
of the tens of thousands of adults and children
who have learned to study and to pray
through the inspiration of the Rebbe *Shlita*
stand him now in good stead,
and may we be soon privileged once again
to hear Torah from his lips
with ever-increasing vigor and joy

*

In Honor of
Shayna Bracha שתחי'
On the occasion of her Birth
2nd Day of Iyar, 5752

*

dedicated by her parents
Mr. & Mrs. Dovid & Sarah Rivka שיחיו Zulauf
& grandparents
Mr. & Mrs. Binyomin & Devorah שיחיו Zulauf
Mrs. Fruma שתחי' Murley
& great-grandparents
Mr. & Mrs. Reuven & Rachel Leah שיחיו Morris